LIFE'S TOO
SHORT
TO FOLD
FITTED
SHEETS

LIFE'S TOO SHORT

YOUR ULTIMATE GUIDE TO DOMESTIC LIBERATION

TO FOLD FITTED SHEETS

by Lisa Quinn

CHRONICLE BOOKS
SAN FRANCISCO

Copyright © 2010 by LISA QUINN.

Library of Congress Cataloging-in-Publication Data:

Quinn, Lisa, 1967-
 Life's too short to fold fitted sheets: your ultimate guide to domestic liberation / Lisa Quinn.
    p. cm.
 ISBN 978-0-8118-6993-5
1. Home economics. 2. Home economics—Social aspects
3. Women—Conduct of life—Humor. I. Title.

 TX145.Q56 2010
 640—dc22 2009025697

Manufactured in China

Designed by ANDREW SCHAPIRO
Cover photo by JEFFERY CROSS
Cover illustration by STEPHEN CAMPBELL

10 9 8 7 6 5 4 3 2 1

Chronicle Books LLC
680 Second Street
San Francisco, California 94107
www.chroniclebooks.com

To all the unbalanced mothers.

TABLE *of* CONTENTS

....

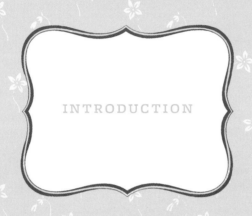

INTRODUCTION

Confessions of a
Disillusioned Domestic Diva

W e've all been there: You abandon your family and spend the better part of the weekend on a complicated décor or cooking project, only to find yourself neck-deep in aioli, sequins, and despair. Perhaps the decoupage bubbled, the soufflé deflated, the paint splattered onto the carpet, or the hot glue didn't hold. Whatever the reason, you are now experiencing full-blown homemaker's remorse: that moment during a project when you have to simply give up and admit that you're in over your head. Have you ever stopped yourself in the middle of one of these household fiascos and asked yourself, "What the hell am I doing here?" Yeah, me too—*hundreds of times*. The good news is there is hope for us all.

For me, it started innocently enough. Decorating, entertaining, and crafting were ways for me to express myself creatively, hobbies if you will. It was all in good fun; I could stop anytime I wanted. *Really*. Over time, however, things began to spiral out of control. I got the monkey on my back. I became a domestic diva.

Good wasn't good enough anymore. In my mind, anything worth doing was worth doing impeccably. My home would be the most chic, and my parties would inspire awe—even if it killed me. It took ten long years of this nonsense before I finally stepped back and took a long, hard look at myself and the insanity I'd created—all in pursuit of perfection.

My big *aha* moment came while watching Martha Stewart fashion a cranberry wreath on one of her holiday specials. She hand-sewed something close to 3,500 *live cranberries* onto a base constructed from sphagnum moss and chicken wire. The finished product was gorgeous; no one could deny its perfection. (Seriously, it was *dope*.) On a normal day, I would have literally sprinted down to Costco for my own 3,500 cranberries, but for some reason, this time was different. For the first time ever, I looked at Martha, *my idol*, and thought, "This bitch is crazy."

Hello, my name is Lisa Quinn, and I am a recovering Martha Stewart junkie. During my decade-long quest to be exactly like her, I built a career as a Home and Garden Television host, author, and columnist. Housekeeping, decorating, crafting, entertaining, and gardening—I had it covered. I shared this wealth of knowledge to hundreds of thousands of loyal fans each week. I'd worked for HGTV, published a decorating book, and even taught Oprah a thing or two about shopping for knockoff upholstery.

But I had a dirty little secret; I was living a lie. Ironically, while I strived to be the perfect picture of domestic bliss at work, I could never quite pull it off in my own home. The daily grind left no time for forcing bulbs, alphabetizing my pantry, scrapbooking, origami napkin folding, or even keeping the house very *clean*, for that matter. I didn't entertain as much as I liked because I dreaded the effort. Hell, I could barely get dinner on the table for my family three nights a week. I was no domestic diva. Instead, I was an overwhelmed working mother of two, and I felt like a complete fraud. It seems so obvious in hindsight, but it was a huge epiphany to realize that maybe I just didn't have the time (or the desire) to keep up the facade anymore. I couldn't help but suspect that other women out there felt as smothered as I did by the pressure to be perfect.

Because honestly, who out there *really* wants to spend an entire Saturday constructing crepe paper peonies for the brunch centerpiece? How does coordinating fancy hand towels with molded soaps (which the family is forbidden to touch) make a home a better place to live? Why are we so uptight about appearances?

Recognizing the problem is the first step to recovery. Whether you like it or not, the truth is simple: We don't slave over all this domestic drivel for our families or ourselves; we do it for the other moms. For us, the Mommy Competition is on, and dammit, we're going to win.

The media bombards us with images of Supermom: this chic Amazon in Jimmy Choos, a baby in one arm, a frying pan full of money in the other. Honest to God, if I hear the words *balance* or *quick and easy* one more time,

I'm going to hang myself. Nothing in those magazines is ever quick or easy. I have tried balancing my kids with my home, my husband, my career, personal hygiene, a social life—and let me tell you, (a) the hygiene and social life lose out every time, and (b) I should have received some sort of honorary certificate from Cirque du Soleil for even *attempting* such a high-wire act. We *all* should. What if we manic moms stopped obsessing over the unnecessary? What if we realized that our value doesn't depend on what other people think? What if we stopped being control freaks? What if we put down the glue gun and got back to our lives? Why, it'd be a revolution, that's what it'd be.

After the cranberry and sphagnum moss episode, I decided it was time to make some changes. No longer would I be a slave to unrealistic expectations of modern motherhood. I would start slacking off, and be proud of it. Instead of constantly overachieving, I would figure out the very *least* I could do to get by without sacrificing style. This new way of thinking led me to discover shortcuts and cheats to pull off the life I wanted, without all the hard labor.

And that's exactly what I aim to share with you. In this book, you'll find an assortment of domestic shortcuts, rationalizations, cheats, compromises, inspiration, contradictions, and confessions to help manic moms everywhere get through the day. It's for women like me who want to entertain and to have the nice house, the clean kids, the decent meal, but don't want to kill themselves in the process.

It's my assertion that the real key to happiness is getting rid of your inner control freak, redefining what's real and important in your life, and then lowering your standards for everything else. We'll begin by discussing perfectionism and how unrealistic expectations negatively affect you and those around you.

Once we've set the bar a little lower, we'll move on to the half-assed homemaking basics: How to give your home the illusion of cleanliness and sensibly chic home décor, and when to just break down and hire a professional. And, finally, don't be the hostess with the most stress: I've included tips for practically effortless entertaining.

I kept it short, because I know you're busy. Perfection is overrated. Live a little.

THE LACKADAISICAL LIFESTYLE

When did life become so complicated? Were our moms this overwhelmed all the time? Were our grandmothers? We over-schedule ourselves, and then overschedule our kids so they can keep up. We have too many choices: stay at home or go to work, paint or wallpaper, private or public, red or white, organic or poisonous? Who really knows?

Overwhelmed and resentful is no way to go through life. We are intelligent, educated women. How did we end up here?

B ack in the 1980s, feminist and editor Helen Gurley Brown said that women could "have it all." It was her good intention that modern *Cosmo* girls could have everything they ever wanted and more: love, marriage, sex, family, and money—you name it, it's yours. So women everywhere donned their best power suits and hit the streets with stars in their eyes. This was the genesis of the great balancing act. Women started making personal sacrifices they'd never faced before: staying late, working weekends, beepers going off during ballet recitals, hiding sick children under their desks, and preparing dinner during conference calls.

Cut to just a few years later, and here comes Martha and her lot telling us that now, on top of everything else, we must be "crafty" too. Store-bought cookies at the bake sale soon became a capital offense. Holidays required mouthblown (you read it right), hand-stenciled Easter eggs and ornate nativity scenes crafted from vintage wood clothespins, embossed velvet, and Chantilly lace. It isn't enough to have a simple tomato plant in the backyard anymore. Noooo, now you must tend to a variety of organic and heirloom vegetables and flowers. You should plant your seeds in the form of a *P* for perfect. This won't be easy to maintain. You will have to prune and fuss with your garden every day for the best results. Oh, and as for your home, it sucks *big time*. Here are some craft and carpentry tasks you will need to perform to stay in the game.

What was once this ideal of empowerment and creativity for women quickly morphed into an evil, unrealistic standard for us all. Perfectionism has now become the norm, and if you don't stack up, well, then, you don't get to play. Women everywhere are racing around, hot-gluing and glittering like drunk monkeys.

The thing about perfectionism, though, is that it's never perfect, right? Things might *seem* perfect for a second, but even then it's only fleeting. It's like the circus performer who spins plates on sticks—one is always about to fall.

Back when I was in the depths of my own perfectionism, people would marvel at my efficiency and attention to detail. That's the thing about this type of obsessive behavior: you build a facade of productivity. I *appeared* to have it all together. For years, I found comfort in the image that I had created for myself: this never-fail, ever-ready mom. HOW COULD THAT BE WRONG? What people couldn't see was that I was doing it for all the wrong reasons, and I was starting to come apart at the seams.

The whole idea of perfectionism is fundamentally flawed. Perfection doesn't even exist. It's a purely mental, alienating, and unnatural state. It just causes judgment and makes people feel bad, so stop it.

AS A MOM, ALSO THINK ABOUT WHAT YOU ARE MODELING FOR YOUR CHILDREN WHEN YOU'RE A PERFECTIONIST:

- You have to blow people away when they come to visit so they will like you.
- Perfectly folded T-shirts and clean faces equal the perfect family.
- You have to kill yourself to prove to others that you've made it.
- A spotless house is more important than fun.
- Work is more important than family.

Here's the brutal truth, ladies: you can't have it all. Why would you even *want* it all? Consider the alternative for a moment. Consider a life without all this pressure. Imagine having happiness, order, peace, and success in your life without all the drama. It begins by stepping away from perfectionism.

Please note: I'm not sure you can totally cure perfectionism. It's more like joining a 12-step program and it is almost impossible to quit cold turkey. I have backslid at least four dozen times since I started writing this book. Just try and take it one day at a time.

S o many of the women I meet say they just want a happier, simpler life. They want to slow down and enjoy more. But when I pressed them about what they could do to achieve that simpler life, I usually get a bunch of blank stares and the occasional lottery reference. No one knows where to begin. It begins by getting your priorities straight.

SET YOUR INTENTION

You can't be passive about success in your life. Later in the book, I'll show you how to create a comprehensive plan to achieve harmony in your home. In life, you should also devise an overall plan. Otherwise, you're only drifting at sea.

Intention is the process of creating a clear vision of what you want in life, opening your mind to the possibilities, and then following through. Simply stated, intention is faith. Call it faith in the universe, faith in a god, or just optimistic faith in yourself. Whatever it is, it seems to work.

I have a great mommy example for this: did you ever watch *Finding Nemo*? Do you remember the part when Nemo's dad hesitates about jumping into the East Australian current to save his son? The surfer turtles are in there anglin' the tasty waves and encouraging Marlin to join them on their path. "It's bitchin', dude!" Marlin is afraid. He worries that he may become injured or lost. He frets that he's not strong enough to ride the current. He fears that it will all happen too fast. There's this moment when you're certain he's going to turn back in defeat, but instead he suddenly jumps right in. He was afraid, but he did it anyway. He trusted that it was all going to work out, and it did. Loosen your tight grip of control and start to roll with the current, baby.

INTENTION BOARDS

It's so easy to default to pessimism. We all gripe about something: we're working too hard, our coworker is an asshole, the house is always a wreck, we're broke and can't afford the things we want. Dwelling on the negative is a direct flight to anxiety and depression. Imagine what would happen if you made a small daily ritual of positive thinking every day. Do you think it would have an effect on your attitude and the way you interact with others?

You may be familiar with feng shui intention collages, or vision boards. These visual wish lists are usually constructed from magazine clippings glued to a poster board. The clippings represent the desires you have for your life. You can use photos, drawings, phrases, whatever works for you. Creating an intention board lets you actively participate in the making of your future. The board forces positive, hopeful thoughts into the forefront of your mind, which in turn promotes real change. Add to the board when you can, and take some time to look at it every day for best results.

I personally like to use a metal bulletin board with magnets instead of the more permanent glued version. The impermanence of the magnets allows me to change out my ideas more easily. Right now I have a huge photo of Oprah right smack in the middle of my board (I kid you not). *Oprah . . . you will love this booook. You will have me on your shooow . . .*

GRATITUDE JOURNALS

I started keeping a gratitude journal online because it was more convenient for me than the traditional, handwritten variety. It still works. I try to write in it at least once a week. It's amazing what you come up with after a while. Keeping any sort of written note of thanks around reminds you of your treasures and also reminds you that there are so many who have less. Acknowledging gratitude makes you a more empathetic and enthusiastic person.

HERE'S A SAMPLE OF A FEW THINGS ON MY CURRENT LIST:

- Healthy, funny, smart, adorable children
- The amazing man in my life
- Family
- Great friends
- My AAA card
- Ice-cold margaritas with salt
- Choice
- Health
- A job that I thoroughly enjoy most of the time
- Locks on bathroom doors
- Having lots of love in my life
- The opportunity to express myself
- Unstructured time
- Gift cards
- The kissies game
- Washing machines
- My daughter's knock-knock jokes
- The crayon drawing of Godzilla v. Mothra left on my desk this morning
- GPS devices
- Netflix
- Grocery delivery
- Amy and David Sedaris
- Living in San Francisco
- Second chances
- Noise-canceling headphones

FYI: The best time to compile your list is when you're stuck in traffic or performing mundane, somewhat unpleasant tasks at work or around the house. Reminding yourself how lucky you are to even have a home can make housework much less dreadful.

I met a busy mom of three just the other day. We were discussing playdates and what a pain in the ass they can be. When you have babies, you just hang out with your other friends who have babies. As the kids grow older, however, you're sometimes stuck having to deal with their friends' parents. If the parents are cool, it's not a problem. If they're not, well, you get the picture.

In the midst of our conversation, this mom said something I found both startling and sad. She said she sometimes skips out on playdates altogether because she feels that her clothes and the clothes of her kids don't measure up. She was embarrassed and felt compelled to spend money she didn't have to keep up appearances. Let me add that this woman was very stylish and in my opinion "had it going on." She was no slag.

I had a similar story to share. I bought a fake Chanel bag once, for certain occasions. I was always terrified that someone with a real Chanel bag was going to out me. It wasn't enough that I was bright, outgoing, and personable; I apparently needed a $2,500 purse, too.

It's not just fashion; it's everything. You've got to love the little zingers you get from the other moms who *just want to help*. "Oh . . . so you send Gillian to preschool. . . . Well, I'm sure that makes it so much easier for you," or "Wow, you let him *eat that*?" or "Bless your heart, you're working so hard. It's no wonder you can't keep the house up." My favorite is, "You look so tired." How do you even respond to that? Should you *apologize*?

What's funny is this never happens to men. Most men seem to have a Teflon coating when it comes to criticism. I've never seen, not one time, my husband come home from work in tears because someone made a snide comment about his new loafers. Men don't seem to care about that kind of stuff (well, straight men anyway). Imagine how liberating it would be to not care what anybody thought. To *really not care*.

It's totally possible—it just takes some redefining. Revisit your self-confidence, focus on the positive, and figure out what's really important. I felt like I was lacking something, so I bought a counterfeit purse. When I was toting that fake Chanel bag around, I thought it would impress people. That seems so *bone-headed* in hindsight. Believe me, it's just as stupid to obsess over your appearance, your home, your child rearing, your work ethic, and your entertaining prowess. You are wonderful just the way you are. Listen, those other women are going to talk anyway. Take yourself out of the equation and pay them no attention. (My friend John would say that they're all just jealous bitches. I love him for that.)

I still have that fake purse. It sits on a shelf in my closet stuffed with plastic bags to help keep its shape. I hang on to it to remind myself what a knucklehead I can be.

REDISCOVERING YOUR SELF-ESTEEM

A WISE MAN ONCE SAID THAT IF YOU WANT TO ENSURE HELL IN YOUR LIFE, WORRY ABOUT WHAT OTHER PEOPLE THINK. THE KEY TO SHAKING OFF THE HATERS IS REDISCOVERING YOUR SELF-ESTEEM. YOU'VE ALWAYS HAD IT; IT JUST MAY BE BURIED UNDER A FEW LAYERS OF RUDE COMMENTS AND MEDIA OVERLOAD.

- Remember that everyone is different but equal—that includes you.

- Just because someone has a different opinion doesn't always make him or her right.

- Lose those negative thoughts in your head. You'll never have inner peace if you're constantly repeating crappy comments about yourself. Catch yourself when you utter phrases like, "I'm no good at that," "God, how can I be such a moron?," or "My ass is as big as the side of a barn." Even when you're joking, negativity will do a number on your head.

- Visualize mistakes as learning experiences and forgive yourself.

- You are who you hang out with. Avoid negative, hateful people. That's consorting with the enemy.

- Don't hold grudges. When there's nothing more you can do but get a chip on your shoulder, it's time to move on.

- Realize that no one really knows what they're doing. Take it easy on yourself.

- Educate yourself about your choices. That way, if anybody tries to give you grief, you'll have a good argument.

- Don't weasel out of the compliments people pay you. Women do this all the time. There is no reason to apologize or deflect kind words; you deserve them. A simple "thank you" is all that is necessary.

- Don't put up with bullshit. Not voicing your needs tells people it's OK to treat you badly.

- Make positive contributions to others. This doesn't mean you have to run around like a galley slave. It means that helping others feels good and fills you with value.

- Be proud of yourself and your accomplishments. Celebrate every victory or achievement.

- Use positive affirmations. Think about it: If you can program your mind to repeat negative phrases about yourself, then you can certainly get into the habit of regularly thinking about your gifts (see Gratitude Journals, page 17). This will change your life. Consider using inspirational quotes or images to assist you.

One of the images that I use for positive reinforcement in my own life is a crown tattoo on my wrist. It reminds me that I am the queen of my life. That doesn't mean I expect pomp and ceremony. The tattoo is a symbol of the best that I can be. The queen rises above petty strife. She demands respect, but she's also gracious and ultimately a servant to her fellow man. I strive to be like that every day. Some days are better than others.

My tattoo is like a kid writing on his hand to remember something; I forget otherwise. It may seem severe, but it works for me. You may want to do something less permanent, like putting a sticky note on your vanity mirror. But the idea is the same: remind yourself of your power.

W e've discussed perfectionism, now let's dip our toes in a little guilt. Are you a "yes-woman"? Do you consent without even processing the request? Do you agree to volunteer (again), then instantly dread the whole process? Do you feel guilty when you say no?

"Thinking you are a bad person for saying no is a symptom of the 'disease to please.' Saying yes when you need to say no causes burnout. You do yourself and the person making the request a disservice by saying yes all of the time," says Duke Robinson, author of *Too Nice for Your Own Good*.

Take care of the ones you love and shamelessly deny the rest. It may be difficult at first, but after a while, you'll see the payoff: more time and less dread. Just say no.

HOW TO GET OUT OF SAYING YES:

- Make sure you understand exactly what is being asked of you before you immediately scream out, "OF COURSE I WILL!!" Breathe before you answer. Take a moment to think it through. You may be signing up for more than you bargained for.

- Develop and stick to your own personal rules. If you don't like lending money to people, then don't lend money. It's not *your fault* you can't help; it's just the rules. This way, it's not personal, and hopefully no one gets their feelings hurt.

- Realize your limitations. Set up a date calendar and make sure to schedule unstructured free time for yourself. Don't overschedule into your free time.

- Remember that you have the right to say no. You'll get taken for granted and disrespected if you're always compliant.

- Keep your answer short. Lengthy justifications just make it seem like you're lying. A drawn-out response might also give you time to start feeling guilty and say yes—especially if you *are* lying.

- Be kind but firm when you say no. Wishy-washy responses build false hope. If you're not going to make it to the fund-raiser, say so. People may be depending on you.

- Provide an alternative if you can. Maybe postpone for a week, or refer the requester to someone who can really help.

- Never offer up a service you don't want to provide in the first place. I used to do this all the time. I would offer before the person would even ask. This heinous act of self-sabotage usually happens right at the end of a phone call. You're trying to say goodbye, when you suddenly blurt out, "Well, hey, listen, if you can't find anyone to help, call me back." NO! Don't tell them that! They'll just call you back! For God's sake, don't succumb to your *own* pressure.

- When someone becomes persistent, repeat your position, perhaps in a slightly different way. If they are still persistent, they are not listening. This is *their* problem, not yours.

- When in doubt, make "no" the default. Remember, it's easier to turn a no into a yes, rather than the other way around.

WHEN YOU *HAVE* TO SAY YES

SOMETIMES, FOR WHATEVER REASON, SAYING NO IS JUST NOT AN OPTION. IN THAT CASE:

- Remind them that they owe you one, and hold them to it.

- Put a tough condition on your agreement. For instance, say, "I can help you with your project, but I'm going to need everything from you by tomorrow at 3 P.M. or I'm out."

- Tell the person you'll help *this* time, but make it crystal clear that the two of you are going to need a better plan for next time.

THE FOLLY OF MULTITASKING

Technology has ruined everything. There's no place to hide anymore. Everyone knows you have e-mail, instant messaging, social networks, and Bluetooth, and they all expect instant replies at any hour. In an effort to keep up, we end up multitasking all the time. It's absurd how much we try to cram into a day.

There have been numerous studies on how multitasking really just means you're doing a crappy job in a bunch of different areas. They say the brain has trouble giving 100 percent to more than one task at a time. I'm no doctor, but I can tell you from my own personal experience that trying to juggle too much all the time will make you bat-shit crazy. Just ask my family.

It's my belief that a lot of this overactivity is simply an addiction to drama. I hear so many people complain endlessly about how busy they are. They bitch and moan about it so much that I'm certain they're secretly proud of it. All that hustling around can give a person a false sense of importance. Could it be that you are only busy for busy-ness' sake? If so, maybe it's time to check in with yourself. Are there activities you could erase from your schedule that would relieve some of the stress? Can you be okay with the fact that you don't have to be occupied all the time? Really?

I'VE MADE SOME SIMPLE CHANGES THAT HAVE MADE A BIG DIFFERENCE. CONSIDER SOME OF THESE FOR YOURSELF:

- Every day, pick just two or three important things that really need to get done. These get your undivided attention. Then do your best to get to the small stuff.

- I've told everyone in my life that I answer my e-mail only once a day, even though I still sometimes check it more often.

- **I took my phone number off my business cards. They now have only my name and my e-mail. I did this for several reasons:**
  - * I hate talking on the phone, and it's not really necessary for my business.
  - * Nothing gets lost in translation this way. If there is any communication confusion, I have everything in writing.
  - * Those damn cell phones give you brain cancer anyway.
  - * I can always write my phone number on the card if I choose to.
- **Use two computers if you can. I have a desktop machine for my writing and a laptop for research. Having everything at your fingertips saves time.**
- **Make technology work for you, instead of against you. If your phone, GPS, or computer software is too complicated, opt for a simpler version. Sometimes all those bells and whistles are more trouble than they're worth.**
- **Schedule small breaks, throughout your day, that have absolutely nothing to do with work or chores. Sit down and read an article or just walk into another room and stretch for 5 to 10 minutes to recharge your brain.**

KID-FRIENDLY MULTITASKING

Multitasking is at its worst when you're trying to give your kids some attention and you are completely distracted with work or a chore. Instead of blowing off the kids, include them in your tasks. This simple act shifts multitasking into family fun.

- **Wash the car and sprinkle the kids.**
- **Clean your bathroom while the kids are in the tub.**
- **Use drive time as a chance to reconnect with your child. Turn off the radio and talk.**
- **Cook together. Kids love to participate in cooking, and you've got a better chance of getting them to eat something they helped prepare.**

- ◉ Make decluttering a game. See who can pick up the most toys. Toss stuffed animals into a large basket free-throw style.

- ◉ Use your smaller kids as resistance in your workout. My kids and I play "astronaut." I lie on my back on the carpet with my feet in the air. One of my kids will "mount" with their chest on my feet. We do a countdown as I slowly straighten my legs and raise them into the air.

- ◉ Take your kid to work. It's important to let your child know what you do for a living and how your job relates to the family's well-being. If they just see you on the phone or on the computer all the time, they'll just think you're ignoring them.

TIARA TIME

When my daughter started first grade, we attended parents' night. It was a time to get the scoop on what was expected of our little girl and to meet her new teacher, Ms. Larson. It was an interesting experience, as Ms. Larson was quite a character. She had an artsy, ethereal presence and seemed a little eccentric, in an absentminded professor kind of way. About midway through the evening, she surprised us all by placing a large rhinestone crown on top of her head. She said we should all know about her practice of "tiara time." I was all ears. Tiara time, she said, was the time of day that was all her own, a time when the children were required to participate in silent, independent study and not allowed to bother her *at all*. She needed to get certain things done, so when the crown went on, the mouths shut. She kept it on for the rest of the meeting, and I gotta tell you, I sat up straighter at my little desk. There were some stunned stares and a few grumblings among some of the parents. I, however, got on board immediately. I raced home, jumped on eBay, and bid on the shiniest rhinestone tiara I could find. It arrived 10 days later, and I have never looked back.

In her book *Women in Overdrive*, Nora Isaacs writes, "We live in a culture where we aren't encouraged, either subtly or overtly, to relax or take time for ourselves." We need a break occasionally, and we need to not feel guilty about it.

Tiara time is a win-win. The crown is a very positive symbol; it's *regal*, for chrissakes. As I wear my shimmering headpiece, it reminds me that I deserve this time. Very much like a Do Not Disturb sign, it alerts my kids that Mommy is not listening to any fighting or tattling during this period, and my husband understands that he is in charge until the crown comes off. There are days when I would like to have it permanently attached, but just feeling like royalty for a few hours a week is a good start toward maintaining my mental health.

FYI: Don't confuse tiara time with family time. Family time is great, but this is strictly me time—sans kids, sans guilt. There are so many ways you can treat yourself without huge expense or effort. And this does not include sewing the kids' Halloween costumes or baking brownies for the school bake sale either. These are things to do for *yourself*. I've compiled a list of suggestions below.

So now all you need to do is find a tiara. If you can't acquire a bejeweled one, a paper crown from Burger King works just the same.

TIARA TIME ACTIVITIES:

- ⊙ Organize your picture albums.

- ⊙ Meet a friend for lunch. Or better yet, happy hour.

- ⊙ Sit in a hot tub and daydream about winning the lottery.

- ⊙ Two words: afternoon delight.

- ⊙ Pull out your old CDs (or *albums*, even) and bust a move.

- ⊙ Slow down.

- ⊙ Spritz lavender water in your sheets and take a nap.

- ⊙ Stretch.

- Do crossword puzzles. They help stave off senility.
- Read dlisted.com.
- Plant some seeds or pull some weeds.
- Create an original painting and try to sell it on eBay.
- Read a real newspaper.
- Go bowling during the day when it's cheaper and not so crowded.
- Window-shop online.
- Write in a journal or personal blog.
- Have tomato soup and a grilled cheese in peace.
- Swing on the swing set with your eyes closed. Imagine you're flying.
- Sit on the front porch with a cocktail and watch the people walk by.
- Eat a whole tub of popcorn by yourself.
- Sneak away to a bookstore and read an entire magazine with no interruptions.
- Indulge in guilty pleasures.
- Consider a new hairdo.
- Make an intention collage (see page 16).
- Play with a pet.
- Relish the quiet.
- Head out with a camera.
- Read a book.
- Go into your closet and try to come up with new outfits from your old clothes.
- Take an unnecessary class, like 17th-century woodworking or Muay Thai street fighting.
- Work out.

Staycations ⊱ It can be costly and time-consuming to travel, but that shouldn't mean you can't have some R & R. Turn off the computer and the cell phone, and have some uninterrupted family fun for a long weekend. Visit local museums, or just play in the yard. Don't do any work and don't answer the phone; this *is* a vacation.

Gay men ⊱ Seriously, I am not trying to be sexist or funny here, but I have found that generally a combination of gay men and champagne is the best antidepressant ever.

GPS devices ⊱ Never get lost again.

Cucumber treatment ⊱ This little extravagance can make any day feel like a spa day. Put a couple of slices over your eyes to reduce puffiness.

Coffee ⊱ Not only a great pick-me-up in the morning, coffee makes a super body exfoliant. Mix 2 cups/255 g ground coffee with $^1/_2$ cup/65 g sea salt and 2 tbsp/30 ml massage oil.

www.truemomconfessions.com ⊱ This is a Web site dedicated to anonymous mommy confessions. You won't feel alone after you visit it.

Smiling ⊱ Even when you don't feel like it. Studies show that even forced smiles make people feel happier.

Friend therapy ⊱ Having a good friend who can share your joys and listen when you're a mess is a wonderful gift.

Google ⊱ Seriously, what did we do before Google?

Random acts of kindness » Studies show that those who volunteer tend to report greater levels of health and happiness. Include your kids in philanthropy. It makes them better human beings.

Treats » A chocolate bar, a cocktail, an antidepressant, or a good cry when you need it.

Rituals » Life can seem so out of control when you're busy all the time. Set up personal routines like a moment of daily meditation, a weekly drink with the girls, or maybe just the same coffee drink each morning. Having something constant—just for yourself—will keep you grounded.

Yoga balls » Replace your office chair with a yoga ball. Simply balancing on the ball strengthens your core while you're working.

Doing less » This frees you up for enjoying more.

Practicing empathy » I used to suffer from an extreme case of road rage. I was flipping people off left and right. Why work yourself into a rage that will get you nowhere? Try to remember that we're all here trying to get by, and lose the unnecessary stress.

Massage » Getting rubbed increases serotonin—your body's natural antidepressant.

Finding your passion » Do something you love to do and do it well.

Meditation » Okay, so who's got time for meditation, right? You don't necessarily have to focus on any magical mantras, uncomfortable positions, or overly religious overtones. Meditation can be as simple as daydreaming, or closing your eyes and breathing deeply a few times.

Orgasms » Endorphins and oxytocin galore. With yourself or the one you love—you get the same benefits either way.

Simple pleasures » Sunsets, good food, fresh-cut grass, a warm bed, your child's belly laugh.

NOT-SO-GOOD HOUSEKEEPING

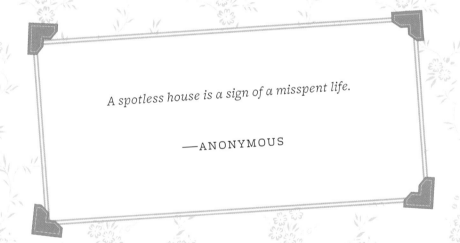

A spotless house is a sign of a misspent life.

—ANONYMOUS

Let's face it: housework blows. Show me a woman who truly enjoys cleaning up her family's filth every day, and I will show you someone who needs to get out more. (Okay, Martha *says* she really likes cleaning, but I'm pretty sure she has hired help.) Magazines, books, and HGTV shows are chock-full of tips for turning housework into a fun, easy, and fulfilling recreational event. They're not fooling me. In this section, I'm going to cover tips and tricks to make your house sparkle without you breaking a sweat. You'll learn about the forgiving properties of low lighting and no-fuss, no-muss cleaning tactics. But before we get into house-keeping shortcuts and cheats, let's first discuss how to avoid a majority of the work from the start. You may not even realize the many ways you subconsciously sabotage yourself when it comes to housekeeping. Read on . . .

We're in the midst of a clutter epidemic. It's compulsive consumption, plain and simple—very much like eating disorders, alcoholism, and drug abuse. The way I see it, a cluttered home is like the path to hell: laid with good intentions, but ultimately ending at eternal damnation. We buy all these things in an honest attempt to make our lives easier and more enjoyable. The irony is that when these things start to pile up, we become slaves to the piles.

I'll admit that when I first heard about feng shui, I thought it was a bunch of hoodoo. "If you place a green plant in the southwest corner of your living room, you'll be rich." Woo hoo! I'll get right on that. However, after further investigation, I discovered that the practice is based on common sense and positive affirmation, not superstition. A particular adage caught my attention. It states that the mounds of unfinished business in your home "scream" at you. Truer words were never spoken. Think about all the time you spend fretting about the clutter in your home. How often do you find yourself shifting piles from one place to another? Are you constantly looking for things that don't have a proper home? It's distracting and adds stress—just as if someone were screaming at you. Feelings of frustration and fatigue are bound to build up over time.

Given this sad state of affairs, people are desperate for organizing solutions, and there's a multibillion-dollar business out there offering solutions. But here's the real truth: There will never be enough vacuum-pack bags, shoe racks, or color-coded plastic bins if your real problem is too much stuff. The amount of time, effort, and money that people spend trying to organize their garbage is unbelievable.

Instead of buying *more* stuff to hold your *existing* stuff, why not just get rid of the original stuff to begin with? It sounds simple enough, but old habits are hard to break. A common rationalization I hear is, "My house is just too small." In a line from Peter Walsh's book *It's All Too Much*, the author says, "Stop saying your house is too small. The amount of space you have cannot be changed—the amount of stuff you have can."

YOU'RE OUT OF CONTROL IF:

- You have more than three "junk drawers."
- You have to navigate piles to get through your home.
- Your closet contains clothes from three years ago—that don't fit.
- All the horizontal surfaces in your home (desktops, countertops, ledges, tables, and mantels) are completely covered.
- Things fall out of your car when you open the door.
- You can't park in your garage.
- You find yourself shuffling piles around all day because they have no real home.
- You have papers from high school.
- You spend an unreasonable amount of time trying to find things in your home.
- You have trouble relaxing or being productive in your home because of the clutter.
- You have unopened mail from months ago.
- You have lids but no containers (or vice versa).
- Your filing system is basically one file, full as a tick, with everything crammed into it.
- You don't invite people over because you are embarrassed.
- You *always* hate the way your home looks.

PARTING IS SUCH SWEET SORROW

Purging can be painful, but it's so important. You will never find sanctuary in a disheveled home. The first step is getting into the mind-set that you are removing your obstacles, not kissing your life goodbye. Next, assess the problem areas and create reduction strategies that are reasonable but effective. Once you start seeing results, you may find the very act of purging an intoxicating experience.

ASK YOURSELF WHY YOU'RE HANGING ON TO THINGS IN THE FIRST PLACE.

⊙ Do certain items have sentimental value but you don't want them out in plain view? Take photos of your objects for memory's sake, place the photos in an album, and then remove the items from your home.

⊙ Are you holding on to an item only because it was expensive? It can be embarrassing to admit you've made a costly mistake, but keeping that item is *another* mistake. Get over it.

⊙ Is there clutter in your home mislabeled as "décor"? Too many knickknacks, throw pillows, and tchotchkes are more shabby than chic.

⊙ Are you hoarding items that you think you may need one day? It's cliché but true: if you haven't used something in a year, lose it.

⊙ Are you just too lazy or too overwhelmed to get started? It's not as hard as you think. Place two large bins, baskets, or bags in your home. Label the containers "Throw Out" and "Give Away." Take five minutes a day to find items you no longer need, and place them in the appropriate receptacle. When the container is full, DO SOMETHING ABOUT IT. If it's garbage, throw it out; if it's donations, put it in your car. (You've got a better chance of getting donations to their final destination if they're with you when you're out.)

⊙ Don't even think about a "Sell" bin. You are never going to get around to selling all that junk. It will just sit there for years. Ask for receipts from thrift stores, so you can write off the donation on your taxes.

ELIMINATE MULTIPLES THAT SERVE THE SAME PURPOSE. ONE OF EVERYTHING IS ALL YOU REALLY NEED.

⊙ Kitchens are notorious for having redundant appliances, gadgets, and food items. Look at your countertops and in catchall drawers for multiple or seldom-used items such as wine openers, whisks, garlic presses, and tomato corers. Unless you're Wolfgang Puck, there is no reason to have three food processors and eight spatulas. Check your pantry for those duplicate spice packets and sauce mixes that get stuck in the back and forgotten.

⊚ Check the countertops, medicine cabinets, and drawers in your bathroom. Seriously, you don't need all those hotel shampoos and samples from the makeup department.

⊚ Inspect your linen closet. Do you have ratty old towels inside that you never use? How many sets of sheets do you own? How many do you actually use? Stick to only *two* sets of white sheets for each bed in the home. White sheets don't fade over time, they're interchangeable, and they're easy to clean.

INSPECT YOUR KIDS' ROOMS. DO YOU FIND YOURSELF ANGRY AND FRUSTRATED THAT THEIR ROOMS ARE ALWAYS A MESS? MAYBE THEY HAVE TOO MUCH STUFF AS WELL.

⊚ Eliminate clothes that don't fit and toys that they don't use. Donate these items to a good charity.

⊚ Traditional toy boxes are black holes. The smaller toys settle at the bottom, never to be seen again. Get the kids a few plastic bins. Divide the bins into categories: stuffed animals, action figures, LEGOS, etc. For smaller children, tape corresponding photos to the bins so the kids know what goes where. IKEA makes a fantastic bin storage system for kids. Don't buy toys with a million pieces. Who are you kidding? It's Murphy's Law: The five most crucial pieces will be lost on the very first day. Then *you're* stuck picking up the other 2,000 pieces, around four a day, for the next 18 months.

⊚ Quit buying little toys for your kids every time you leave the house. It's so tempting to impulsively pick up an inexpensive treat for your kids while you're out. It makes them happy for the moment, but ultimately it's only more clutter.

⊚ Many of us tend to get carried away with the décor in our kids' rooms. Don't make your kids' rooms too fussy. You can't expect your kids to make their bed every day if it's incredibly complicated. Stay away from all the frills like fancy little pillows, throws, and accessories that serve no purpose.

GET CREATIVE AND STAY FOCUSED

Make a great first impression » My foyer tends to be the messiest catchall in my house, and it's the first thing you see when you walk inside. Hang hooks along the wall for coats, hats, scarves, and backpacks. If you have the space, place a small bench below the hooks for easy shoe removal. Store your shoes underneath in baskets.

Trash junk mail immediately » Use magazine files (found at any container or office store) as in- and out-boxes for all other mail. These files come in a variety of colors, and since they are vertical, rather than horizontal and tiered, like traditional mail files, they take up less space on your desk. You can also store your mail on a shelf for maximum desk space.

Shop with intent, not impulse » Always have a list. It's so easy to get carried away and buy that sweater you don't need or those cute candlesticks you have no place for. Or that toy that you're buying simply because you feel guilty that you're not spending enough time with your kid. These things take up space. They will end up gathering dust and getting in the way. Don't set yourself up for failure. Less stuff = a happier life.

Throw a "shaming party" » We don't see our own clutter after a while. Bring in some friends who will have more objective views. Serve some wine and appetizers. After a glass or two, your friends will no doubt have plenty of opinions on what you should lose. Be ruthless. If you haven't used an item in a year, why do you have it?

Don't get discouraged » Just as Rome was not built in a day, all your clutter will not disappear overnight. Keep sorting, eliminating, dumping, and organizing. As you see results, you will be motivated to keep going.

Life is really simple, but we insist on making it complicated.
—CONFUCIUS

As witnessed previously, my rule is, "The less stuff you have, the less you have to clean." Reducing household clutter and *keeping* it out is your ticket to easy street. On that note, the less complicated the items you *do* bring into your home, the less upkeep they will require. Once you rid yourself of the excess clutter in your home, you will need to figure out reasonable strategies to keep your home neat and hassle free (okay, mostly hassle free).

We all make mistakes when it comes to furnishing and appointing our houses. We make impulsive buys, we convince ourselves that we really can keep the kids off the new white sofa, and, worst of all, we never throw anything out. Me? Guilty as charged. In my early days as a set stylist, I would adopt any piece of furniture left over from a shoot. I figured if it was free, how could it be wrong? After a while, my house began to look like the insides of a *Where's Waldo* book. Over the years, I've learned to choose quality over quantity; I've made great strides in streamlining my home and, in turn, my life.

COMMON MISTAKES THAT MAKE YOUR LIFE HARDER AND
YOUR HOME MESSIER

Shopping as entertainment ⚹ We girls just love to shop till we drop, don't we? Stop it! If you are simply buying things because shopping is fun, you need a new hobby. From now on, everything you bring into your life must serve a purpose and have a specific home. Buying something just because it's cute is not reason enough. Give yourself a "cooling off" period. Wait a week; if you still want it, go back for it.

Hanging onto everything » Institute a "one in/one out" policy and stick to it: If you buy something—*anything*—you have to get rid of something else.

Pets » *I know*—all you animal lovers out there are gathering your torches to come after me. It's not that I don't like animals. They are cute and sweet and can bring lots of joy to your life. With that said, many are hairy, stinky, and occasionally lose control of their liquids. If you're thinking about getting a pet—think long and hard about the dander, litter, kibble, and dribble. If you already have a pet, you may consider keeping the pet in designated pet areas to minimize the mess.

Thirteen throw pillows on your bed » You know the look: three European shams in the back, four standard-size pillows in the middle, four fancy throw pillows arranged along the front, and a fringed, heart-shaped pillow up front and center. It's a very fussy look, and *so* 1992. Most people don't even bother to put all the pillows back on the bed unless company is coming. Mounds of pillows end up surrounding the bed like a feather fortress. You step over them every day, and then feel guilty about the mess. Get rid of all of them. Streamline your bed with plain white sheets and a simple duvet or quilt. When you get out of bed in the morning, all you really need to do is straighten the pillows (flat, don't bother propping them up against the headboard *just so*), and fold the duvet over to expose a flap of sheet. Don't obsess over everything being even and wrinkle free. There's something quite sensual about a slightly sloppy bed; it's like tousled, after-sex hair. A tightly tucked, perfectly made bed with 13 throw pillows in neat rows is uptight and prudish. What are you saying about yourself?

Using sponges » They're death traps—well, not really, but sort of. Sponges collect germs down in their recesses, and then redistribute said germs all over your home. That's more like biological warfare than cleaning. Brushes and microfiber cloths are a much better option. If you just can't part with your sponge, toss it in the dishwasher with every load.

Fabrics that need to be ironed » Honestly, I couldn't tell you where my iron is right now. I hate ironing. We are fortunate to be born in an age when we can choose from a myriad of synthetic and wrinkle-resistant fabrics. It's a sin, really, not to take advantage of them. High-thread-count sheets have been the rage for ages, but most have to be ironed. Ironing sheets is a joke, so make sure you choose the right kind. One hundred percent cotton is the softest, but it's going to wrinkle. Most home stores carry at least one line of wrinkle-free cotton sheet sets. These are made from 100 percent treated cotton. The wrinkle resistance in these fabrics will last up to 50 washings.

FYI: Be aware that even "wrinkle free" will wrinkle a little bit.

Kids' clothes are especially ridiculous to iron ⋈ The little maniacs will *immediately* spill something on themselves, and then you're stuck doing laundry and ironing again. Stick with wash-and-wear, and save hours on laundry each week.

Unrealistic ideas about your décor ⋈ Face it: The kids are not going to stay off the sofa, your husband will eventually wipe his dirty hands on the fancy guest towels, the dog will chew the legs on the Chippendale dresser, and white carpet is for masochists. If your décor style conflicts with your lifestyle, you will always be frustrated. See more about "reasonable" décor on page 44.

Using fabric softener on towels ⋈ It certainly sounds like a good idea to put softener on towels—fluffy comfort after a bath, right? Wrong. Fabric softener (both liquid and sheets) reduces the absorbency of your towels and leaves your skin feeling slightly slimy afterward. Really.

Buying in bulk ⋈ You can save a lot at those big "club" stores. The problem is, once you get home with all your bargains, you've got to store all those monstrous packages somewhere. At the very least, consider buying regular-size products for those that are seldom used. Seriously, who needs four gallons of mayonnaise? If there's no place to store it, don't buy it.

Overhead lighting ⋈ Only turn on your overhead lights if you're looking for something small, like a contact lens. A darker room *looks* cleaner. Use lamps and dimmers on all your overhead switches.

Buying your kids too many toys ⚹ There's a saying, I'm not sure who said it, but it's absolutely true: "The more the toys do for the children, the less the children do with the toys." Stop buying the latest fad toys for your kids. They inevitably end up discarded in a corner of their room, ignored and taking up space. Don't feel guilty. We've all heard, "But Mommm, every-one else at school has one." Make your kids go out to play. They'll get some exercise and fresh air. They'll be more creative in the long run, and you'll have less to climb over every time you enter their room.

Cleaning up after your kids (and/or husband) ⚹ How many times have you said to yourself, "Oh, it will just be easier to do it myself!" when refer-ring to household chores already assigned to someone else? In her book *When Organizing Isn't Enough*, Julie Morgenstern says, "If you find your-self picking up toys or washing the dishes when you've already delegated those tasks, stop. Taking over other people's chores sends the signal that it's all right to be lazy." With that said, getting children to actually pick up after themselves can be an exercise in futility. Instead of yelling, "GO CLEAN YOUR ROOM!," ask your child to perform a series of smaller tasks. Children can be overwhelmed with large jobs, especially if they don't understand how to stay organized and focused. Challenge them to first pick up all their books and put them in a basket or small hamper. When they have finished that, send them off to perform another job such as plac-ing all their stuffed animals in a designated bin, and so on. Make sure to congratulate your child after every task is completed. Kids thrive on posi-tive reinforcement (as do husbands).

A great tip for helping smaller children stay organized is to set up a "photo bin" system. Organize their toys into a few groups: stuffed animals, action figures, Barbies, etc. Provide baskets or bins for each category. Tape a photo of the corresponding toy onto each bin so the child understands what goes where.

Now that you've learned some of the common mistakes to avoid, it's time to get down to the fundamental rule of housekeeping: your home doesn't have to be clean to look clean.

THE TOP 10 THINGS YOU HAVE TO CLEAN— IN ORDER—IF COMPANY IS COMING IN 30 MINUTES

A home should be as clean as you can get away with.
—SHIRLEY CONRAN

You know the scenario: Friends are coming over, and you've procrastinated all week and haven't cleaned the house. Now you're wigging out because you've got less than two hours and nothing to show for yourself but a sloppy house and an empty pantry. This happens to me almost every other weekend, so I've compiled a handy check-off list for speed cleaning. It covers exactly what needs to be done to make it look like you live a neat and tidy life. My husband and I try to beat our old record each time we entertain. Our best time—for everything on the list—is 17 minutes. I am NOT kidding; we are like a friggin' pit crew. Make sure to enlist your husband and kids to help; it's their house too.

LAST-MINUTE CLEANING CHECKLIST

 The Toilet ⊳ At some point, somebody's going to need to pee. The toilet needs to be *spotless* if company is coming. Keep disinfecting wipes in your kitchen and baths; they're great. Like baby wipes, all you do is rip them out of the tub and wipe—instant shiny and clean. Run one over your sink, then hit the seat of the toilet (don't forget the underside). Check the mirror. Empty the wastebasket. Check for any hair on the floor. Run a wipe over the worst—who's got time to mop?

BTW: All of the eco-companies are coming out with their own versions of nontoxic recycled or recyclable wipes, so don't feel so guilty.

② Clutter ‣ I try to keep some sort of basket with a lid in every room. IKEA makes a big basket "trunk" that can serve as a coffee table and a clever stash spot for toys and blankets. Scan all the horizontal surfaces in your home. Are any of the surfaces cluttered with old mail, remote controls, dishes, and homework? Loads of clutter makes you look like a total slob, so this is a priority. If you're in a real pinch, grab a trash bag or laundry hamper. Load it with your clutter, and hide it in a closet. Don't forget that the dishwasher and oven work well as temporary stashes for dirty dishes. Just don't forget to empty out the clutter when the guests leave.

③ Floors ‣ This is the area where you can probably cut some corners. I find that running a vacuum over the carpet *and* floors is just fine. If you've got any sticky spills, hit them with some spray cleaner and a Swiffer-type mop. Another option is to spray some cleaner on two rags. Throw them on the floor, and get your kids to skate around on them instead of using the mop. Concentrate on the high-traffic areas only. Remember, we are cutting corners here; if you're lifting furniture or getting on your knees at any point, you're over-doing it—take it down a notch.

④ Excessive Dust ‣ A little dust is fine; no one sees it but you. However, if it's come to the point where the dust is thick (perhaps the children have scrawled WASH ME on the dining table), it's time to grab a duster. It's always a good idea to polish your finer wood pieces with quality wood oil when you can, but for those in-between times, I find a feather duster works just fine. For the half-assed housekeeper, it's the perfect tool. The beauty of the old-school duster is that it's much more a redistributor of dust than a true cleaner. It gets rid of *enough* dust so that you won't notice the spots you missed, and you save valuable time because you can just dust around those pesky knickknacks, frames, and vases without having to lift and move them. If you have allergies, there are loads of disposable dusters on the market. They do a superb job of removing the dust in a hurry. You can also use facial tissues. You have to use the ones with lotion. Puffs and Kleenex both carry tissues with lotion. Great for your nose, great for dusting in a pinch.

(5) **The Fridge** ❧ If you are having a dinner party, someone is bound to ask if they can help and reach for the refrigerator. This is one place where clutter and disorganization is fine, but sticky grossness is not. Clean any puddles or drips with a swipe of disinfecting wipe, and dump any suspicious-looking leftovers.

(6) **Mirrors** ❧ Slightly dusty or filmy is fine, but if you have fingerprints, smudges, or splatters, grab a bottle of glass cleaner and a microfiber cleaning cloth. Microfiber cloths don't leave streaks and can be washed and used over and over again.

(7) **Cobwebs** ❧ Check ceilings and light fixtures. Chandeliers can be the worst offenders, so double-check that dining room fixture before the dinner party.

(8) **Your Bed** ❧ In a perfect world, you would make your bed and tidy the bedroom. But let's face it, you probably don't have time for this. If you find yourself strapped for time, just shut the bedroom door (and lock it).

FYI: This plan will not work if you are having guests over for the first time. They always want a tour. See page 38 for my simple bedding and bed-making advice.

(9) **You** ❧ Save primping till the end. All that speed-demon housework is bound to wreck your look. You want to be ravishing, so better to freshen up afterward. However, feel free to move this step up if you're running out of time.

(10) **The Final Touch** ❧ Spray a fine mist of nontoxic spray cleaner in the air *right by the front door*. You didn't really clean anything, but it *smells* like you did. Remember, perception is reality.

INTERIOR FINISHES THAT HIDE THE MOST DIRT

Housework can't kill you, but why take a chance?
—PHYLLIS DILLER

U nless you can afford daily maid service, it's impossible to keep a house spotless all the time. However, there is a way to have a cleaner-*looking* home. It's all about smart shopping and avoiding the pitfalls that can make housekeeping more difficult. Choosing elements for your interior design should be as much about function as form. That sleek black velvet sofa you loved in the store? It will be a magnet for lint and hair. Silk is delicate and hard to clean, laminate floors scratch easily, stainless steel shows every fingerprint and scratch, and you can't clean wool carpets with bleach, ammonia, or heat. The good news is that there is a plethora of other finishes that are easy to clean and hide the dirt you *can't* clean. Here is a list of the best and worst finishes for busy family life:

PAINT

There are five main types of paint finishes: flat or matte, eggshell, satin, semigloss, and high-gloss enamel. Flat will hide the most architectural flaws, such as cracks, small dents, or poor spackling jobs. It's warm and beautiful, easily my favorite finish. However, it's the most difficult to clean (meaning, it's impossible to clean). Satin and semigloss are the easiest to clean, but they can illuminate every flaw in the room. An eggshell finish is a good compromise: it hides minor flaws and wipes clean. Gloss finishes are best on doors and trim because they're the most durable.

FLOORING

One of the most unfortunate design mistakes I ever made was when I chose the flooring for my first apartment. I decided to tile the entire space in black and white squares. Very French, very chic, I thought as I lugged all 400 vinyl tiles into the living room. And it was indeed, *très* chic. That is until about five minutes later, when the dust started to settle. The black tiles showed all the white dirt, and the white tiles showed all the black dirt. You should have *seen* the look on my face. Heed the suggestions below when choosing flooring for your home to save yourself the tears that I shed on that dark and dusty afternoon.

CARPET

Let me preface by saying I hate carpet. Think about what carpet really is: It's a sponge that wipes off the bottom of your gross shoes when you walk into the house—*ew*. Bacteria can grow in carpet and cause discoloration and odors in your home.

Avoid or rip out carpet altogether when you can; institute a no-shoes policy if you can't. Because guests always seem to be a little thrown by a no-shoes policy, include a heads up in your invitation. Keep several pairs of cheap flip-flops or slippers in a basket by the front door, so everyone has house shoes.

If you must go with a carpet in your home, pick a medium-toned, multi-tonal Berber, commercial grade, or low-pile shag. These types of carpet will hide dirt and wear in high-traffic areas. Ask your dealer about any stain protection plans offered. Consider investing in a good steam cleaning two or three times a year to extend the life of your existing carpet. Remember: Dirty carpet looks disgusting, and there's no hiding it.

If you find yourself with carpet stains, I always suggest you go green first. I've listed a few homemade concoctions on the following page using items from your pantry. That said, if you have a tough stain, you might need to bring in the commercial, store-bought cleaners. There are loads of eco-friendly cleaners out now that actually work.

STAIN TYPE

⊚ Cocktails or beer ⊚ Dirt/mud

⊚ Berries or jam/jelly ⊚ Milk/yogurt

⊚ Cola ⊚ Washable ink or marker

⊚ Poop ⊚ Wet latex paint

⊚ Ice cream

Make your own cleaning solution of one part white vinegar to three or four parts water, and keep it under your sink in a squirt bottle. Spray onto the stain, and let it get good and saturated before wiping (scrubbing) with a clean white rag.

STAIN TYPE

⊚ Blood ⊚ Vomit

⊚ Tea/coffee ⊚ Wine

⊚ Mustard ⊚ Chocolate

Mix 1 tbsp/15 ml ammonia with 1 cup/240 ml water. Apply with a squirt bottle; remove by wiping (scrubbing) with a clean white rag. Just like bleach, ammonia can remove the color from a wool carpet. If you have a severe stain on a wool carpet, call a professional.

WAX OR OIL

Place a paper towel or paper bag over the stain, and iron on warm setting. The offending spill should transfer from the carpet to the paper.

GLUE

Most water-based glues can be removed with a little rubbing alcohol. Moisten a cotton ball or soft cloth, and blot the dried glue. Once the glue residue is saturated, gently wipe it until it's all gone.

GUM

Use ice to freeze the gum and then smash it off with a mallet or butter knife. Make sure you get all the pieces off the carpet before they start to thaw.

URINE

Absorb as much as possible with towels, and then blot with a damp cloth. Next, spray a solution of one part white vinegar to one part water over the affected area. Blot with towels until it's as dry as you can get it.

FYI: Carpets with stain protection must be cleaned with certain products formulated just for them. Make sure you know which cleaners you can use or risk voiding your warranty. These "special" cleaners are clearly marked and can be purchased anywhere you buy household cleaners.

HARDWOOD FLOORS AND LAMINATES

Hardwood floors and laminates can be a good thing or not, depending on how you live. These very versatile materials seamlessly coordinate with any décor, they're easy to clean, and they look great. However, the new trend of dark walnut finishes will show every piece of lint that falls on them. Be prepared to Swiffer every day (like that's going to happen). Choose oak or pine floors instead; the busier grain will camouflage the dirt. Hardwood also scratches, so if you have kids and pets, look out. Laminates give the look of a hardwood floor—well, sort of. They are much less expensive than wood, and there are a lot of beautiful "faux exotic woods" out there, but be warned: most laminates scratch easily. A dab of polyurethane applied with an artist's brush will disguise most small scratches. For deeper gashes, grab your kids' crayon set. Find a coordinating color, and slice some slivers into the crack. Melt with a hair dryer, and buff with a cloth.

EASIEST TO MAINTAIN

- Stone or tile (if sealed properly)
- Cork

- Hand-scraped hardwood (this is an uneven, more rustic version of hardwood flooring found at any flooring store; because of its somewhat jagged, worn appearance, it is better at hiding scratches and spills)
- Marmoleum and linoleum

To hide dirt between cleanings, you want a flooring material that has some randomness to it. An all-white (or black-and-white) tile floor is *crazy*, but Mexican Saltillo tiles, slate, cork tiles, or an old-school speckled linoleum will disguise most small spills, rogue Cheerios, and scuffs. All of the listed choices are easy to clean: vacuum, sweep, and/or mop using a mild detergent and water. Wood and water don't mix. Use specialized wood cleaners for hardwood flooring.

UPHOLSTERED FURNISHINGS AND TEXTILES

The light cottons, velvet, and suede are the absolute worst fabrics for families. Light, solid cottons will show every hint of dirt, velvet attracts hair and lint, and suede is impossible to clean. Following are the most durable, easiest-to-clean fabrics; but that doesn't mean they're indestructible. Heed these cleaning rules to add years to your furnishings:

LEATHER

I will tell you right now that the key to a happy home is brown leather. It's tough and hides dirt better than any other textile. Although more expensive than fabrics, it's the best investment. There are many different varieties, with varying textures and durability. Darker, neutral tones hide the most dirt, but should you get a stain, try one of these solutions:

Water stains » Allow the wet area to dry naturally—no hair dryers. Apply a good leather conditioner once the area is *completely* dry.

Grease » Blot the area, and apply a coating of cornstarch/corn flour. Let it sit for three to five hours, and wipe off.

Ink ⁛ Dab a small amount of rubbing alcohol onto the stain, then wipe it off with a cloth. Ink is not easy to remove. You may need to call in a professional.

VINYL

Considered the ugly stepsister of leather, vinyl is much less expensive but is less attractive, colder to the touch, and less durable. That said, if you are looking for a budget-minded fabric that is super-easy to clean, vinyl is the answer. Wash with a mild detergent and water. Avoid abrasive cleaners, as they can scratch the smooth surface.

FYI: If you have kids, this might be the only way to get a white sofa in your living room.

MICROFIBER

Liquids bead up on microfiber, making it easier to wipe up spills (if you get to them right away). That doesn't mean you can use simple soap and water, however. Although liquids will bead on microfiber, once a liquid has soaked into the fabric, you will be left with a permanent water spot. Instead of water-based cleaners, dab or blot a bit of ammonia or rubbing alcohol onto the spot. Vodka works, too.

There are many products on the market specifically for cleaning micro-fiber. Ask your dealer if you're buying new.

CHENILLE

Chenille combines beauty, durability, and softness. Lightly vacuum every couple of weeks to remove dirt and dust that can get stuck in between the fibers. Most companies offer stain protection on chenille, which allows most liquids to bead up so they can be cleaned before the stain sets. Clean set stains with a mild detergent such as an upholstery shampoo. Test the cleaner on an inconspicuous area first to check for bleaching. Flip your cushions reg-ularly to prevent uneven wear.

SLIPCOVERS

Did you know that reupholstering your furniture is insanely expensive—often more expensive than buying new? It's true. Unfortunately, desperate people all over the country have resorted to using store-bought, "one size fits all" slipcovers to extend the life of a torn, stained, or just plain ugly sofa or chair. It's my opinion that the makers of these slipcover products should be sued, class-action style, for false advertising. The *idea* of a slipcover is a good one. The name really says it all, *slipcover*. You simply slip a piece of fabric over your ugly sofa, and voilà, it looks stylish and brand-new. If you've ever tried wrestling one of these bastards onto a sofa, however, I'm sure you agree that they should be called damned nuisances.

You never know which end is the front, they never fit right, and you end up re-tucking, yanking, and pulling on it every time someone stands up. Oh, and God help you if you need to wash the cover. The wrinkles get so deep, your sofa looks like a gigantic khaki raisin.

The only slipcovers I have found that work are the ones that are spe-cifically made for that particular sofa. Pottery Barn and IKEA have a nice selection. Pay close attention to the washing instructions, or they'll shrink. Air-dry, and invest in a steamer to smooth out the wrinkles. Keep in mind that cushion covers will never look the same after they are washed. Over time, most will lose their shape and fade, and you'll never get all the wrinkles out. Dry-cleaning is a more costly alternative but will add years to the life of your slipcover.

APPLIANCES

Stainless steel is all the rage, but it will show every scratch and fingerprint. It is gorgeous but a total pain if you have kids or pets. However, certain appliance brands offer similar finishes that are easier to maintain. Clean Steel and Platinum Stainless are some trade names to look for. Black-and-white finishes are classic and the easiest to keep clean.

Whether it's outdated information or just a hack trying to sell you something, there's a lot of bad information out there concerning housekeeping. Here is a list of my favorites:

Myth #1: You must fold your fitted sheets ⚹ The real definition of insanity is folding a fitted sheet the same way over and over again and expecting it to result in anything other than a migraine and a huge turban. Quit stressing about it. Just wad it up the best you can, and shove it in the closet. Most of the wrinkles stretch out when you put the sheet on the bed, anyway.

Myth #2: Bleach cleans everything ⚹ Bleach is an excellent disinfectant but not a great cleaner. While it kills germs, you need to scrub and rinse surfaces for the best cleaning job. Add to that the fact that bleach is toxic. It smells terrible and can irritate the skin, eyes, nose, throat, and lungs. Mixed with other cleaners that contain ammonia, it can be lethal if inhaled. Many green companies are coming out with nonchlorine bleaches. Natural borax works wonders on whites in the laundry.

Myth #3: Newspaper cleans glass ⚹ We're all trying to recycle, and there was this rumor out there for a while that using recycled newspaper with your glass cleaner leaves a streak-free shine on your mirrors and chrome. The truth is newspaper can leave ink smears all over your glass and hands, and certain inks contain toxic ingredients. There are so many better ways to recycle paper these days. Don't reuse it in your home. Invest in a microfiber cloth instead.

Myth #4: Hairspray will remove ink from upholstery ⚹ This used to work back in the day when they loaded hairspray with alcohol. These days, hairsprays contain little or no alcohol, so they don't work. Use undiluted rubbing alcohol instead.

Myth #5: More soap = more clean ✻ When going for that super-clean feeling, sometimes we think we should load up on the soap. If a little soap works, shouldn't a lot of soap work even better? Actually, no. Excess soap is difficult to rinse off and can leave a slightly slick or sticky residue. This residue will attract even more dirt, especially on floors.

Myth #6: Your kids' rooms have to be spotless ✻ It's their room, for crying out loud. Obviously we don't want an avalanche every time we open the door, but slight chaos is fine. Cut 'em some slack.

Myth #7: You have to use furniture polish every time you dust ✻ Over-doing the furniture polish will actually cause a waxy buildup that attracts even *more* dust. An in-between feather dusting is better for the furniture and easier for you.

Myth #8: You have to spend one whole day cleaning everything ✻ Instead, try tackling one small area twice a day. Unload the dishwasher while your coffee brews in the morning; fold laundry during a favorite TV show. Consider a "one room a day" cleaning regimen. Just 10 to 15 minutes in a room can make major changes.

Myth #9: You need a different cleaner for every surface in your home ✻ Sure, there are surfaces that need special cleaners, like stainless steel and granite, but the truth is you can clean most surfaces with a simple glass cleaner and a microfiber cloth. Check under your kitchen sink for redundant cleaning supplies that are taking up valuable space.

Myth #10: You have to scrub your floors ✻ Rubbish. Spot cleaning is fine if you stay on top of it. Vacuum your floors when you're vacuuming your rugs. This will keep the floors tidier between cleanings. Only when necessary, perform a proper mopping with a real mop and a bucket.

Myth #11: Housework is women's work ✻ Make your family help. Threaten them if you have to.

AGE-APPROPRIATE CHORES FOR KIDS

2–3 YEARS OLD

- Pick up toys and clothes.
- Feed pets.
- Put away some groceries.
- Help make beds.

4–6 YEARS OLD

- Water plants.
- Help sweep and mop.
- Unload the dryer.
- Dust.
- Fold washcloths and hand towels.
- Empty the dishwasher (what is within reach). Make it a household rule that whoever cleans up after dinner can choose the dessert.

7–10 YEARS OLD

- Prepare for school (brush teeth, comb hair, get dressed, make cereal).
- Make her own lunch.
- Make his own bed and change the sheets.
- Mop, sweep, and vacuum.
- Make snacks for younger siblings.

11–15 YEARS OLD

- Cook.
- Babysit.
- Mow the lawn.
- Take out the trash.
- Wash the car.
- Clean the bathrooms.

16–18 YEARS OLD

- Face it, these kids are practically out the door. They need to be able to do everything: balance a checkbook, clean the house from top to bottom, maintain their own car, care for siblings, buy groceries, run errands—*everything*.

DELEGATION

"If you want the job done right, do it yourself." Are you familiar with this old saying? Of course you are. Perfectionists want to do everything themselves, right? Why would you ever leave a job to someone who's just going to screw it all up? How could that be effective?

Problems arise when perfectionism begins to block the path of productivity. Case in point, you can spend so much time and effort trying to do a task *just perfectly* that the job never actually gets completed. You have to get over the fact that no one will do certain tasks exactly like you would. The new motto in our house is, "It's better than good; it's done!"

If you're feeling overwhelmed with responsibilities, get help. If you can afford it, consider hiring a college student to run errands and watch the kids. They are cheap and can usually be flexible with their hours. If your family is not pitching in enough, tell them there is a new sheriff in town. Break down responsibilities and assign tasks accordingly. It may be a pain at first, constantly reminding everyone of their new chores, but stick with it. You'll be glad when you wake up one day and realize you're not doing everything anymore.

DO'S AND DON'TS FOR DIPLOMATIC DELEGATION

DO wait to provide feedback until after the task is finished. Discuss what was good and what could have been done differently for better results.

> FYI: You catch more flies with honey than vinegar here—stay positive.

DON'T micromanage. If you're unsure of a person's abilities, start small with one task. Don't nag or assist—that's more dictating than delegating. Be very clear about the results you want to achieve, so there is no confusion from the start.

DO get your kids to pitch in. We moms very often get into the habit of just picking up after everybody. Don't coddle your children. Hand them a broom.

Rain-X ✂ Original use: helps rainwater slide off windshields for better visibility. Wipe it all over your glass shower doors every month or so. You'll never have to squeegee again. Pick up a bottle at your local auto store.

Cheap flip-flops ✂ Use them as house shoes for you and your guests. A shoe-free home is a cleaner, healthier, and *less-vacuumed* home.

Lint brushes ✂ Keep one in your car, one at your office, and a half dozen stashed around your house. They also make great lampshade dusters.

Working in teams ✂ Ever notice how professional cleaners always show up in a group? It's because they get it done faster that way. Enlist your husband to help you make a bed, and get your kids to wipe down the counter while you scrub the tub.

White candles ✂ Original use: romantic mood lighting. Rub them on your bathroom grout to prevent mold and mildew.

Alka-Seltzer ✂ Alka-Seltzer will clean a dirty vase or a ring in the toilet bowl in a pinch. Just drop in the tablets and watch them work.

Mr. Clean Magic Eraser ✂ If you have kids, you need this. It will take almost anything off almost any surface. It's particularly good for crayon marks on walls.

Ice cube trays ✂ Not just for the freezer anymore. Place one in a dresser drawer to keep your earrings separated. Use a plastic silverware divider for your necklaces. They work as well as a proper jewelry box, and they don't take up as much space.

Paper plates » You eco-nuts can yell at me all you want. Every now and then, it's nice not to have to do dishes.

Extra socks » We've all got the little pile of socks with no mates. I don't mean to beat a dead horse, but seriously—where do those socks go? Place a small basket near your clothes dryer for all the lone soldiers. Slip one over your hand and use as a "dust glove." They work great on candlesticks, lamps, lighting fixtures, and small accessories.

O Mop from Method » It's an eco-friendly Swiffer basically (the mopping pad is washable and biodegradable). I love it for spot mopping, which—let's face it—is the only kind of mopping I really do.

Aluminum foil »

- Remove dirty buildup on the face of your iron. Simply lay out a piece of foil, and iron it. The buildup sticks to the foil.

- Sharpen your scissors. Grab scraps of foil, and cut through six to eight layers; your scissors will be like new.

- Prevent nasty spills in your oven. Line the bottom of your oven with a sheet of foil. This will save you the laborious task of scraping off all the burnt-on gunk afterward.

Salt »

- Prevent ants from entering your home. Ants won't walk over salt, so sprinkle it over doorways and windowsills.

- Help clean spills in your oven. If the potpie overflows, pour salt over the mess. The salt will halt the burning smell and form an easily removable crust over the top of the spill.

- Place artificial plants in a large bag with salt. Shaking the bag will remove all the dust from the leaves and flowers.

Plastic cutting boards » *I know*, the wooden ones look so much prettier. They're also harder to clean and harbor bacteria. If you like the look of butcher block, buy one. There are gorgeous ones out there. I have a large basket-weave bamboo board that I use when entertaining. It makes the perfect presentation for breads, fruits, and nuts. However, for chopping, I only use plastic. Just throw it in the dishwasher, and you're done. No fuss, no muss, no worries, no oiling.

Baking soda/bicarbonate of soda ✻ Replace all of your abrasive, powdered cleaners with baking soda. It's inexpensive, safe for the family, and works great on sinks, tile, and grout.

A basket with a lid in every room ✻

- In the bath, fill a small basket with rolls of toilet paper so no one's left high and un-dry.

- In the living room, use a larger basket for kids' toys. Young ones will procrastinate taking toys to their room, but you can make it easier for them by setting up a small basket in the rooms in which they play.

- In a bedroom, consider the storage baskets that slide under your bed. Store seldom-used items in these baskets, as you're not going to want to get on your hands and knees every time you need something. Store out-of-season clothes there. This will lessen the load on your closet, so that you can actually find your in-season clothes.

- In other rooms, a covered basket is a great place to stash items you can't find a proper home for—things you occasionally use, like blankets, photos, kids' artwork, office supplies, and seasonal décor items.

Crayons ✻ Crayons are usually the *cause* of housekeeping problems, but if you have scratched hardwood floors, the brown ones are godsends. Grab your kids' crayon box, and pick out a color similar to the color of your floor. Fill in the scratch, and melt the wax with a hair dryer. Buff with a cloth.

Facial tissues with lotion ✻ These make awesome dust cloths. They pick up dust and lint off your furniture just as well as those more expensive Swiffer dusters. Grab them in a pinch.

Worcestershire sauce » Didn't use a coaster and now you've got an ugly white ring? Rub a little Worcestershire sauce into the ring, and let it sit for a couple of hours. Wipe it off with a rag.

A cleaning bucket » Most of us don't have storage space to keep cleaning items in every room, so consider buying a bucket. Keep your sponges, rags, and cleaners inside. It's a mobile cleaning station.

Citrus peel » Next time you're making margaritas, throw the lemon and lime peels (in small pieces) down the garbage disposal. The peels not only make your kitchen smell great, but they also help maintain the integrity of the disposal blades.

Baby wipes » The best product ever invented.

Paintbrushes » Not just for artistic expression, paintbrushes are great at getting the dust off the top of your baseboards.

Essential oils » Most room deodorizers you buy at the major chain stores contain harmful chemicals. A better way to freshen up a room is to put a few drops of essential oil on a burning lightbulb. The heat from the bulb allows the fragrance to waft throughout the room.

White vinegar » It will clean almost anything in a pinch. Mix it with water, and keep it in a spray bottle under your sink.

A flat iron » Yes, the one for hair. You didn't hang up your shirt properly, and now the collar has a huge wrinkle in it. You're already late. What do you do? Warm up the flat iron. It's quick and easy for small ironing jobs.

Dishwasher-safe glasses and dishware » Never buy anything you have to wash by hand.

Shout Wipes and bleach pens » For those of you out there who haven't discovered these gems, they are these pocket-sized miracle workers that instantly remove most small stains in your clothing. They will save your life if you get a lunch stain on your lapel right before a meeting. They can also help you get extra wears out of your garments in between laundry days.

SLACKER CHIC

There was a time when I would buy *Domino* at the newsstand even though I knew it was coming in the mail any day. I literally could not wait three days for my subscription to arrive. Very much like a tween with *Tiger Beat*, I tore the pages out of *Architectural Digest* and taped them all over my walls. I was *obsessed* with *Elle Decor* and *Dwell*. Sound familiar?

I'll still thumb through one of these magazines while in line at the supermarket, but the love affair is mostly over. They started to bum me out. Let's be honest: These magazines set a pretty unrealistic standard for the rest of us. Instead of filling me with creative inspiration, they did a much better job of making me feel like I lived in a total dump. It never failed; I always liked what I saw in the magazines better than what I had in my home. There was this constant need to upgrade.

Having your head filled with too many idealistic images can intimidate even the most confident decorator. I'm not saying you should run out and cancel all your subscriptions. These magazines hire the greatest minds in the business and can offer loads of creative inspiration. You simply need to be realistic about their content. Remember: Just as we're told not to compare our bodies to the wafer-thin models in fashion magazines, you can't reasonably compare your apartment to Elton John's St. Bart's retreat.

Magazines and decorating shows hire entire crews of people to construct, clean, stage, steam iron, and professionally light those rooms. Cameras lie and Photoshop enhances. It's literally that one second in time, as the flash fires, that this "perfect" room is captured for eternity. Before and after that moment, the room is a hot mess. Trust me, I used to be a set stylist for HGTV. It's all smoke, mirrors, and duct tape. (For more on the magical uses of duct tape, see page 96.)

When all we ever see is this type of unrealistic imagery, it's no wonder we become disheartened when it comes to our own home décor.

Over the years, I've met hundreds of women who say they feel completely lost when it comes to decorating their homes. These tortured souls tend to fall into two distinct categories: Those who are too overwhelmed to do anything but wring their hands and apologize, and those who are in manic overdrive, tweaking and re-tweaking, and then maybe just re-tweaking a little more. I get it. No one wants to live in a hovel, but continual fretting and fussing is not the answer; neither is ignoring your space and hoping it'll fix itself on its own. We need to find a happy balance here, and the good news is it doesn't have to be difficult.

First, some tough love: You can't simply click your heels and wish for great design. You need a plan. Now, don't freak out. Forming a comprehensive decorating plan is easier than you think. And I'm going to show you exactly what to do. You don't have to take an AutoCAD class at the local community college or buy a drafting table. You are simply required to approach your home with purpose, not endless swings and misses.

We're going to be taking baby steps, so don't feel like you have to perfect your whole house at once. Trust me, if you start feeling overwhelmed, you'll never finish anything. Focus your energy on one room at a time, and try not to move on to another project until you are completely finished.

The goal is to create a lovely environment, not a second job. A home should be simple, comfortable, and easy. Who wants to be Little Miss Fuss-budget anyway, always straightening and primping? Slacker chic happens when you have made it work, when you are finally at peace with the design of your home. Half of that peace comes from doing the job right. The other half comes from not caring what other people think. I'll help you with both.

In my dozen years as a designer, I've learned some tricks that I'm going to pass on to you here. In this section, you'll learn how to approach a room from a fresh perspective, clear your space, use what you have, determine color palettes, and, most important, accept what you can't change. Let's get started!

SLACKER CHIC 101

GETTING STARTED

First of all, shake off the fear. You are a smart, creative, and innovative person (and people like you). You can do this. Remind yourself that this is not brain surgery. The key to easy and livable yet stylish design is simple preparation.

My first and most important piece of advice: Don't dawdle.

Give yourself a strict time limit. True story: I honed my lightning-fast decorating skills as a set dresser for makeover television programming. Each week, I was allowed 24 hours to completely make over a room—clearing out the space, preparing a design, painting, shopping, delivering, assembling, accessories, artwork, *everything* in that short amount of time. I completed 294 rooms with one assistant. I'm not bragging here; that was an insane thing to do, and it almost killed me. What I am saying is that sometimes *too much time* can leave you with too many opportunities to change your mind. Going with your gut is really the heart of design, so listen to your inner voice; it's usually right.

AN OUNCE OF PREVENTION

My mother-in-law has a needlepoint pillow in her home. It's very funny. It reads, "Plan ahead," but the *e*, the *a*, and the *d* are all squished together at the end. The needlepointer obviously didn't practice what she preached. Think long and hard about that pillow as you prepare for your décor project. Instead of running out and impulsively buying whatever you see, begin by taking an inventory of what you already have. Next, consider how any new items you introduce will work with those existing pieces. Creating a simple step-by-step plan will ensure things go more smoothly for you than with that pillow.

Don't go trying to confuse slacker chic with lazy decorating. Anybody can do nothing. What I am suggesting is a new way of thinking about your home. Instead of falling into the perfection trap (where everything has to be arranged *just so*), consider this brilliant revelation: maybe it's not cool to be perfect. Maybe it's not cool to match the pillows to the carpet to the curtains to the molding. Maybe, just maybe, it looks like you're trying too hard.

Finding inspiration for your décor can be as simple as browsing fabric stores, furniture stores, and flea markets. Furniture retailers hire professional merchandisers to style their showrooms. You can learn a lot about color trends, furniture arranging, scale, proportion, composition, design styles, and accessory placement by simply window-shopping at Anthropologie. If you can't get out, peruse art, furniture, or interior design Web sites and magazines. There are also dozens of wonderful decorating blogs out there that specialize in igniting your creativity. The beauty of the Internet is that you can find inspiration while simultaneously giving the appearance of working.

When professional interior designers begin a project, they usually create a "concept" or "sample" board for their client. Obviously, it can be quite difficult to visualize a finished product in an empty room, so these boards help the designer tell the story of how all of the elements in the room will work together. I strongly suggest you start a sample board of your own. This doesn't have to be a difficult or time-consuming project. The board can be as simple as a few paint chips and fabric swatches stapled to a piece of paper. This will allow you the ability to test new colors, fabrics, textures, and ideas before you commit. When you see all of your ideas laid out in front of you, you can sense what is creating interest and what's not working at all. It's easier to trade out items, and introducing new ideas is made much more convenient. It won't take long to see your project take form.

FYI: Never buy fabric, flooring, or paint on your first visit. Ask for samples of paint and carpet and swatches of fabric so you can see what they look like in your home. Take a long look at the samples in natural light and then in the evening with artificial light.

FINDING YOUR STYLE

I've watched the decorating shows and read the magazines that offer helpful tips on how to find your style. They say it's as simple as looking in your closet, gathering inspiration from a trip to Tuscany, or visiting a five-star hotel for the latest trends in sleek and modern design. Wow! That sounds easy!

Be warned: it's not always that easy. In theory, one should be able to decorate with an idea in mind. You can be inspired by certain design styles and decorative images. However, when deciding on a specific look for your home, you need to be realistic. Consider the architecture of the room, your existing furnishings, and your lifestyle when choosing your "style." Just because you like something doesn't necessarily mean it's going to work in your house.

Case in point: You will never have an authentic Mediterranean villa look if you live in a split-level ranch with blue wall-to-wall carpet. It's simply not going to happen. Even in the best-case scenario, it's just going to look like a store in the mall that *sells* Mediterranean décor.

Sometimes you have to give up the dream. In my own home, I've had to dramatically scale down my ideal design style. You see, I'm a huge fan of delicate Asian antiques, vintage silk draperies, hand-scraped hardwood floors, and hand-knotted Turkish wool rugs. I'm also broke and have two kids under the age of 10. I'm sure you can see where this is going.

Chaos rules at my house. I don't have the energy to fight, so my kids are climbing all over the house all the time. Out went my vision of fine silks and antiques, and in came the distressed pine, dark brown leather, and IKEA—*lots* of IKEA. And guess what? It looks great.

I was able to put my own spin on rather practical furnishings, and I'm very pleased with what I see. More important, I don't have to scream at my family every time they touch something. Not everything in your home has to be super-exotic and -expensive to be fabulous. If you're married with kids and pets, work full-time, and occasionally eat in the living room in front of the TV, I'll tell you what your design style is: it's rustic—intentionally or not.

Finding your style should be as much about how you live as what you see. Accept that and decorate accordingly.

YOUR ROOM PLAN

I t's easier to think of decorating a room as a series of manageable layers, each one complementing the others in an intentional way.

LAYERS OF DECORATING A ROOM, IN ORDER:

1. Clear your space

2. Compose the color palette

3. Use what you have

4. Change what you can / accept what you can't

5. Organize textiles (window treatments, upholstery, rugs, etc.)

6. Create storage

7. Choose lighting

8. Add artwork, accessories, and small details

CLEAR YOUR SPACE—FIRST YOUR MIND, THEN YOUR ROOM

Earlier in this book (page 32), we talked about the importance of removing clutter from your home. (This is going to be a prerequisite for any attempt at décor, by the way.) The next step is deciding which room will be your first victim.

Many designers say that you should start with the master bedroom. Their theory is that if you have a beautiful, restful sanctuary, you will be in a better mind-set to take on the rest of your house. That's cool, but I tend to think that since you're conscious more often in the other rooms of your home, you should start there. But hey, it's your call.

Now comes the part where I ask for the leap of faith: Once you've chosen a room to redecorate, move everything out of it. I mean everything; I want that room empty. Yes, I understand that this seems like a whole lot of work for a chapter titled "Slacker Chic," but you have to trust me here. If you want dramatic change in your space, you will need to see your room with a more objective eye. This is practically impossible if you don't empty the room first. For instance, if your fuchsia papasan chair has always sat next to the wall with the window, it will be hard for you to see it anywhere else. This lack of vision can put a major monkey wrench in your creativity. But if space allows, I *suppose* you could be a little less enthusiastic and simply move your larger furnishings into the center of the room. We are slacking, after all. Once the room is cleared, study it the way a painter eyes a blank canvas, and see the possibilities.

QUESTIONS YOU SHOULD ASK YOURSELF WHILE STUDYING YOUR BLANK CANVAS:

- What are you going to be doing in the room? (Entertaining, resting, working, reading, eating, etc.)

- Are you keeping most of your existing furnishings, or are you buying new?

- What, if anything, will you donate or discard?

- How do you entertain? Casually around the kitchen island? More formally in a well-appointed dining room? With bean dip and Diet Cokes on TV trays?

- Can you paint the room? (Renters, beware: Landlords usually *flip out* over this, so make sure you have permission beforehand.)

- Could you use more storage?

- Do you have kids and/or pets?

- Will this room serve double-duty? (Home office/guest room, dining room/sewing area, etc.)

- Have you thought about a color scheme?

- Of the existing furniture and accessories, do you know what you really like and really dislike? (Be bold. Eliminate the items you don't like as soon as possible. They will only cramp your creativity.)

- Most important, what is your budget?

Enlist a friend or two to help. They can help keep an eye on the kids, give you a second opinion about where your furnishings should go, and even assist with any heavy lifting. (I would at least provide the girls with a cocktail and some snacks afterward for their trouble. Make a little party out of it.)

COMPOSE THE COLOR PALETTE

Before you get started on a color scheme, I highly suggest you buy a fan deck from your favorite paint store. A fan deck contains every color the paint store carries. These decks come organized and indexed for easy reference, but you have to ask a salesperson for one. They cost about $20, and all the major paint companies sell them. Interior designers carry a fan deck with them at all times, and you should too. Keep one in your car until all your projects are completed. You'll be surprised at how often you use it.

Next, take an inventory of the furnishings, textiles, and accessories you're certain are going back into the room. Do you have any favorite pieces? The easiest way to build a color scheme is to pull the colors for the room from multicolored area rugs, draperies, patterned upholstery, or large artwork and build on those.

Your fan deck should act as your color reference guide throughout your entire decorating project. For instance, if you're out shopping for artwork, and accessories, you can't lug a huge sofa cushion with you, but you can match the color of the sofa to a paint chip in the deck.

One of the biggest mistakes people make when choosing a color palette is not knowing the difference between a background color and an accent color. You may love red, but bright red can overpower a room, especially if your furnishings and accessories are deep tones as well. Getting a room right is a lot like putting on your makeup. Your foundation is the neutral backdrop to the dramatic pops of color like eye shadow and lipstick. If you choose a subtler wall color, this will allow your favorite colors (in textiles and accessories) to stand out. The result is generally much more pleasing to the eye than an overload of bright, rich color everywhere.

Bright colors can get old after a while. If you don't want to repaint often, choose muted, more neutral colors on your walls. Subtle tones are a sophisticated choice that will also stand the test of time. If you need a change, simply introduce colorful accessories and textiles or perhaps an accent wall.

PAINT

Paint is by far the easiest, least expensive way to make dramatic change in your home. It can add color and character, and it can even give the illusion of space and architectural detail.

That said, you know that chirpy little person who tells you, "Hey! It's only paint! If you don't like it, just repaint!" Well, that person has no intention of helping you repaint. Seriously, I would like to address that theory. Painting is a huge pain in the ass. Who wants to go through life repainting rooms? We've all been there, that moment right after a long day of painting, when you look up in horror to discover the paint on the wall looks *nothing* like that stupid little paint chip in your pocket. Friggin' agony, that's what I say. Pick the right color the first time, and be done with it.

FINDING AN INSPIRATION PIECE

This is really the only reliable way to pick a color, so it's the only way I'm going to address. Use a multicolored textile, like an area rug, drapery, throw pillow, or duvet cover, as your inspiration palette. You'll be safe selecting a coordinating paint color from the background of the print. Use the deeper or brighter tones for accents throughout the room or in adjacent spaces.

Most paint stores now offer a color-matching service. You can bring in just about anything, and they will match the color perfectly.

For help choosing paint finishes, go to page 44.

COMMITMENT ISSUES

Live with the color before you commit. Instead of buying an entire gallon of a color that could be wrong for your room, purchase several small samples of the colors you're seriously considering. Benjamin Moore, Glidden, and Devine Color offer samples, usually for around $5. These inexpensive samples will cover about a 2-ft/60-cm square. But here's the trick: don't paint the walls. Instead, paint a poster board from the craft store. Tape the board to your wall, and live with it for a few days until you have a strong sense of how the color will look in the room. If you don't like it, just rip the poster board off the wall. No commitment; we like that.

A big mistake people make when choosing colors is going too pastel with their choices. I had a girlfriend who called me once in a panic. I made a "house call" only to discover her in a puddle on the living room floor. She'd picked three paint colors and proceeded to paint her foyer, living room, and kitchen. The foyer was mint green, the living room was baby blue, and the kitchen was soft pink. It looked like the Easter Bunny lived there. She had no idea what she'd done wrong but knew enough to know it was really bad. When you're looking at those paint chips, don't immediately opt for the paler colors. Work your way down the chip to the more intense hues. Choose more muted colors that contain brown or gray undertones for the best results.

THE SLACKER CHIC PAINT JOB

Now that you've chosen a color, you want to make sure the paint job looks professional (note that I said "looks" professional).

Opt for a good-quality paint ⁕ You may pay a few more bucks for the paint, but higher-quality paints are thicker. This minimal investment can save you the agony of having to paint a second (or third) coat.

Use a tarp ⁕ Everybody thinks they can get away without a tarp. You almost always end up dripping. It takes more time to fuss over your drips than to drag an old sheet or towel out from the closet. Save yourself the trouble.

Get a good brush ⁕ Purdy makes my favorite brush. These brushes have such a precise edge that I rarely need to tape anything. This saves a lot of time.

Stay away from dark tones, especially red ⁕ Dark colors take way too many coats. You will see spots you missed for *years*.

Never paint a ceiling ⚭ I know, they say you can make a room more spacious by lightening up the ceiling with paint. I admit they're right, but OMG is it a pain. Unless your ceiling is navy blue or stained, it's usually not worth the effort.

If you really need to paint a ceiling, use a tarp, a small ladder, and a roller with an extension bar. Try to match the ceiling color to your trim (that way you don't have to tape it off).

Paint barefoot ⚭ That way, if you step in a drop of paint, you will feel it before you track it through the house.

USE WHAT YOU HAVE

Unfortunately, not all of us can start from scratch when it comes to a decorating project. A budget-friendly way to get out of a decorating rut is to simply rearrange and repurpose the furnishings and accessories you already own.

- ⊙ **Get a new perspective by arranging your bed against a different wall. Waking up to a fresh view in the morning might make you feel like you're in a new room.**

- ⊙ **If you have a large living room, pull your furniture away from the walls to create more comfortable, cozy seating areas. If the room is small, consider placing some pieces on the diagonal to add visual space.**

- ⊙ **Repurpose, reuse, and recycle items from your home for a brand-new take on accessorizing.**

  - * Clippy rings make it possible to hang just about anything from a curtain rod. You can find them anywhere that draperies are sold. Consider hanging saris, large vintage maps, or quilts. For an exotic or old-world feel, move a Persian rug from the floor to the wall by hanging it "tapestry-style" from a curtain rod. Just be warned: a rug is heavy. If you want to hang one from a rod, make sure the rod is securely mounted.

  - * Transform a folding floor screen into a headboard by simply placing it against the wall behind your mattress. (You may need to tack it to the wall with screws to avoid having it crash down on your head in the middle of the night.)

* Shorten the legs of an old desk to make a coffee table.

* Hang dishes as artwork. You don't need to choose interesting patterns—or even color, for that matter—a group of white plates against a darker wall makes a smart, graphic-inspired look.

* Add casters to an old steamer trunk to make a coffee table with an eclectic/industrial feel.

* Reupholster barstools with old sweaters. Simply cut the torso out of the sweater and apply a felt backing with spray adhesive.

* Use old record album covers as art by tacking them to the walls with fancy upholstery tacks.

* Flip an unused bookcase on its side for a new TV stand or sofa table. Attach casters or inexpensive screw-on legs (found at any hardware store).

* Use a rusty wire gate as a fireplace screen.

* A colander makes a whimsical lampshade for a kitchen or dining room.

* Dress up a plain picture frame by gluing a vintage rhinestone brooch onto a corner.

⊙ **If you don't have any of these items lying around, they can all be found for cheap at salvage yards or at online auction sites.**

CHANGE WHAT YOU CAN/ACCEPT WHAT YOU CAN'T (OR DECORATING AROUND THE UGLY STUFF)

My husband and I bought a Craftsman-style house once. We wanted it more for the trendy neighborhood than the actual structure. Nothing against Craftsmans, it's just never been my style. The rooms were small and had old, very dark paneling three-quarters of the way up the walls. The windows were also small, and most didn't open. It was like the Bat Cave—except without all the cool gadgets.

I wanted to paint the wood paneling. My dear husband, however, was *vehemently* opposed. "It's *Douglas fir*, for chrissakes!" he would shriek at me any time I broached the topic. "We'll lose our investment! It's *old school!*"

I would like to add that his precious Douglas fir was also warped, sun-bleached, and beat up, but I digress . . .

In the interest of picking my battles, I decided to try and make our home seem more light and airy with certain furniture, textile, and accessory choices. After all, I was a professional interior decorator. If anybody could make it work, I could.

It didn't work. Ever. I am not lying to you; I must have changed my mind 200 times over the six years we lived in that house, and I never got it right.

After six years, we put our house on the market. Our Realtor gave us an estimate of what we could expect to get for it. He also hinted that a lighter look might make the home more appealing. That's all I needed. I begged my husband to let me put a few coats of bright white semigloss over that beat-up wood paneling. He relented and I had the whole house painted. I kid you not: it was *amazing*. That dank hellhole was instantly transformed into an open, airy, adorable cottage. The paint cost $150. How much time and money had I spent fighting that dark paneling over the years? My husband, ever the jokester, wondered aloud why we hadn't painted earlier. I resisted the urge to strangle him, and we sold the house in 10 days. My only regret was that I never got to live in that cute cottage. All I got was the Bat Cave.

I guess the moral to the story is that you should never listen to your husband. Well, that and "When your house gives you lemons, make lemon drops."

MAKE IT WORK

⊙ If you're stuck with ugly wall-to-wall carpet, blend similar tones throughout the room, *even if you're not crazy about the color of the carpet.* You don't have to use a lot of this color, but you should sprinkle shades of it throughout the room for a balanced, intentional, more harmonious look. It's no use trying to pretend you don't have the carpet. Attempts to cover it with brightly patterned rugs will just magnify the problem. Consider a neutral, monochromatic look for your rugs, wall color, and larger furnishings to neutralize the room. Purchase artwork, throw pillows, accessories, and curtain panels in more appealing shades of the offending color.

- Do you have an awful brick wall or fireplace that you're too nervous to paint? Do you try to hide the brick behind random artwork and accessories? How is that working for you? People are so afraid they're going to ruin the architectural integrity of a home if they paint brick. Here's the thing: that's only if the brick is totally awesome. If your brick is cheap, nasty, and/or sooty, paint will only improve it. (See how to pick a paint color on page 71.)

- Got obnoxious furniture you can't afford to replace? If it's made of wood, consider painting it. Sometimes it's not the shape of an item but the color that is off-putting, and paint is cheap. If the offending piece is a large upholstered item, refrain from drawing more attention to it by adding extra-busy pillows or crazy-patterned throws. Think of these heinous pieces like you would a tantruming child: the less attention you pay to it, the better. Choose a minor, less offensive aspect of the furnishing, like an accent color or texture. Repeat that color or texture throughout the room for a more harmonious look. (Read why slipcovers never work on page 50.)

- You can't have an airy "spa feel" in a 5-by-8-ft/1.5-by-2.5-m bathroom with maroon tile, so quit trying. Eliminate excessive decorations like large shells full of sea sponges, dozens of (rarely used) candles, and stacks of towels. This is not a spa, it's a *tiny bathroom*, and all that stuff is making it feel even more cramped. Streamlined is better in small spaces. Use solid white shower curtains, towels, and washcloths to brighten the space.

- Create the illusion of larger windows. Hang your curtain rod higher and wider than your window. When you attach the curtains, the window will appear wider and taller.

- Old brass chandeliers and wall sconces can make your home look dated. You may not know that you can easily paint them. Remove and clean the fixtures. Apply a primer made specifically for metal, and then paint the fixtures any color you want. Black is always a good choice; it's a classic. When my daughter was a baby, I painted the brass chandelier in her nursery hot pink. The juxtaposition of the old-school shape with the contemporary color made for a delightfully whimsical touch. Also consider those small lampshades they make for chandeliers. Cute shades can dress up any old fixture.

- ⊚ **If your landlord won't let you paint:**

    * Pull together textiles, accessories, and artwork that contain shades of white. This will make the wall color look more intentional.

    * Dozens of companies now offer fabulously chic wall decals. You just peel and stick. When you're ready to take them down, they peel off with no damage to your wall.

    * Simple, neutral-toned furnishings and loads of black-and-white photos in matching frames will give your room a sleek gallery feel.

- ⊚ **Got hideous kitchen cabinets? I never suggest painting as a quick and easy way to spruce up your kitchen, because it is a lie. This task is far more challenging than you may even imagine. It's a time-consuming, expensive, and filthy job. The results are almost always anticlimactic, and the doors will stick every time you open them. I've been a professional decorator for more than a decade, and I can't even get professional painting companies to paint cabinets for me. Instead, upgrade your cabinets by trading out the old hardware for new knobs and drawer pulls. Simply replacing the knobs on your kitchen and bathroom cabinets can make a huge difference with minimum effort.**

    * There's an old saying in design, "If you can't hide it, celebrate it." To minimize the impact of ugly kitchen cabinets, choose wall paint and accessories that complement the cabinets instead of competing with them. An intentionally designed room will always look better than a failed attempt at ignoring the elephant in the room.

    * Anthropologie sells gorgeous knobs, but they can be pricey if you're replacing a lot. Check eBay or your local salvage yard for less expensive versions. They may not all match, but that could be part of the charm.

SCALE AND PROPORTION

Does your minuscule coffee table get lost between your monstrous sofa and chair-and-a-half? How about that painting behind the sofa? Does it seem too small for the room? Then you might have scale and proportion problems.

It's important to pay attention to how elements in a room relate to the size of the room (scale) and to each other (proportion) in terms of size. For instance, a huge sectional sofa with large, rolled arms would be out of

HOW TO MAKE A SMALL ROOM LOOK LARGER

It's hardly ever the case that people have too much space. Very few of us need to scale down the look of a huge mansion. Instead, we need tips and tricks to make a small room feel larger.

HERE IS A LIST OF MY FAVORITES:

- A room with too many furnishings looks cramped. Use multi-functional furniture such as a chest or basket that can double as a coffee table, storage ottomans, sofa beds, platform beds with drawers, and so on. Use an extendable dining table with leaves, folding tables, or nesting tables, which can be tucked away when you're not using them.

- Make sure the scale of the furniture fits the size of the room and that the lines are clean. Choose sofas, love seats, and chairs with exposed legs. Big, clunky furniture takes up space, literally and visually. Choose a glass table, which will give the illusion of open space. This allows light to filter under the furniture, making the room appear lighter and roomier.

- Place your furniture on an angle to make a room feel larger. The longest straight line in any given room is the diagonal. When you place your furniture at an angle, the arrangement leads the eye along the longer expanse, rather than the shorter wall. You also get the bonus of being able to stash items behind the sofa.

    FYI: This only works if your furnishings are somewhat smaller in scale. Huge sofas on the diagonal eat up too much space.

- Consider making a few of your larger furnishings, like armoires and bookcases, the same color as your walls. This allows these behemoths to blend into the room and visually widen the space. You can add some detail by adding a few colorful accent accessories on the shelves.

- If the furniture in your room is very tall, it can give the illusion that your ceilings are low. Remember scale and proportion in small rooms.

- Don't block passageways. When large furnishings and accessories block the view into your room, the area seems crowded. By moving furniture back and away from walkways, you'll open up the space and make it feel larger.

- It's a bit of a myth that dark colors make a room feel smaller. The bigger culprit is too many colors and too much contrast. Small rooms need an element of calm. Go darker if you like, but stick with a low-contrast, monochromatic color scheme in the room.

- Open up a room with light-colored flooring. An easy way to lighten up a floor is with an area rug.

- Avoid heavy, drapey window treatments. They eat up space and block natural light from entering the room.

We've already talked about this at length, but I'll say it again: Don't go crazy with accessories. They can make a room feel closed in.

scale in a small sitting room. Likewise, a petite settee is dwarfed in a large, open family room. People tend to make the biggest mistakes when choosing accent pieces like occasional tables, accessories, and artwork. Remember: A few large pieces look better than a smattering of smaller items.

The general rule is that everything you bring into a room should be scaled to the size of the room and proportional to the other items in the room. I agree with the rule most of the time. But it's not like it's the law of gravity. You're not obliged to obey it all the time. Sometimes an oversize painting can add drama to a small space. Play around a little and do what works for you.

ORGANIZE TEXTILES

Textiles can make or break a room. Because they are generally the items that bring color, texture, and pattern to the space, it's important that textile choices follow a plan. Too few patterns and textures and it's boring; too many and your home might look like Pee-wee's Playhouse (which is absolutely fine if that's what you're going for).

AREA RUGS

When possible, make the area rug your first purchase when decorating a room. An area rug anchors a room and can make coordinating the space a whole lot easier. Use the rug as a guide for your color palette, by pulling the colors from it for your furniture, paint, and artwork. A well-chosen area rug will coordinate patterns, furniture, and artwork to complete your room design.

Color

Dark, deep-toned area rugs add warmth and can make a room feel cozier, while light or brightly colored rugs can open a room and provide the illusion of space. If you're working around existing furniture pieces, make sure to bring your swatches to the rug store to ensure coordination.

FYI: Super-light or -dark solid rugs show dirt easily. Medium-toned, patterned rugs are the easiest to maintain.

Pattern

When choosing a pattern for your area rug, consider the other textiles in your room. If the color palettes are similar, you can mix patterns. However, make sure to balance intricate patterns with less complicated designs throughout the room, so your room doesn't look too busy and jumbled.

FYI: Busy patterns hide all sorts of dirt, stains, and lint.

Material

Will the rug be placed in a high-traffic area? Will children and/or pets be wallowing all over it? You may want to invest a little extra money in a higher-quality rug that will be more durable. Ornate, multicolored rugs are better at hiding stains and wear. Synthetic rugs aren't nearly as "cushy," but they are the least expensive, hold up to almost anything, resist fading, and are the easiest to clean.

Sizing

Determining the size of your rug will depend on a number of variables. The scale and proportion of the rug in relation to the room and the other furnishings are crucial.

- Arrange your furniture before choosing the size of a new area rug. A room can look more pulled together if all of the legs of the furniture are sitting on a room-sized area rug. If you go with a smaller rug, make sure all the legs are *off* the rug. Half on/half off looks awkward.

- For larger rooms, you have two options:

  * Choose a large rug that allows for even borders (at least 18 in/46 cm) from rug to wall.

  * Choose several smaller rugs to delineate the different living spaces in a single room. It's fun to mix and match here, but don't get carried away. Drastically different colors and styles will be jarring to the eye.

- For smaller rooms, the general rule is to stay away from bright colors and intricate patterns, but go with your gut here. Allow at least an 8-in/20-cm border from rug to wall.

- For a dining room, calculate the size of your rug by adding at least 4 ft/122 cm to the length and width of your dining table. This will ensure that the table and all the chairs sit comfortably on the rug—even when the chairs are pulled out.

- An area rug will look more even if it sticks out at least 18 in/46 cm from the sides of a king- or queen-size bed. For a twin, the rug should extend at least 1 ft/30.5 cm from the sides of the bed. If you have a bigger room, you can go for a larger rug, but don't go any smaller or it will look strange.

FYI: If you're fussy, stay away from area rugs that have fringe on the ends. This fringe can drive you to drink. I used to try and comb them straight; they would stay that way for about 45 seconds. The messy fringe will mock you every time you enter the room.

UPHOLSTERY

I have a strong opinion concerning major upholstery purchases. These are your investment pieces, and they should all be neutral solids. Seriously, save the funky fun prints and florals for your accent pieces like rugs, pillows, and draperies. Trends fade, and you don't want to be stuck with a $5,000 paisley sofa that you can't afford to replace. If you have kids, pets, and husbands, go for solid neutral leathers, vinyls, or microfiber—they're the most durable and easiest to clean. See page 48 for more information on durable fabrics.

DRAPERIES AND WINDOW TREATMENTS

I believe it was the renowned designer Barbara Barry who said draperies shouldn't look like prom dresses. I couldn't agree more. Forget the sashes, swags, puddles, tassels, and the custom fabric. First of all, it's just too difficult to pull off that look properly. Second, those swoopy curtain styles are magnets for dust. Last, but most important, these styles just look dated and ridiculous unless you live at Graceland.

Think about what window treatments are really supposed to do: They block the sun, provide privacy, and maybe add a little pizzazz to your walls.

Keep it simple. If you prefer a modern design, or have kids and/or pets, you may want to consider eliminating long, flowing draperies altogether. Instead, explore the vast array of inexpensive, ready-made miniblinds and Roman shades available at most home stores. When choosing wood blinds, match their color to your trim color for a custom look. Avoid vertical metal and paper blinds if you can; they are just awful.

If you prefer the softer look of drapery panels, you can find loads of ready-made versions. Then personally "customize" these store-bought draperies by attaching ribbon, beads, buttons, or small silk flowers. I have had great success coordinating throw pillows with draperies by attaching matching decorative trim to both.

The window itself may be the most important part of the treatment. If you want to make a window seem larger, run the curtain rod past the window, along the wall. You can de-emphasize an unattractive window by choosing a fabric that won't stand out against the wall color. Mounting draperies as close to the ceiling as possible will make the ceiling seem higher.

As with every other textile element in your decorating plan, you need to consider all the other colors and patterns in your room before you choose a window fabric. Collect swatches for your sample board (see page 65) before you buy.

Accent Textiles

This is the area where you can have the most fun and get a little trendy. Accent pillows, throws, dining chair cushions, and table runners are relatively cheap and can be returned easily if you don't like them once you get them home. Pull the brighter colors from your existing draperies, rugs, and large upholstery pieces for your accent fabrics.

Fabric and home stores usually group their textiles into collections. They create combinations of large prints, smaller patterns, florals, stripes, and solids. This "Garanimals" approach to décor can make the job of coordinating a whole lot easier for the novice decorator. Bring your sample board with you the next time you hit the stores and spend some time deciding what works and what doesn't before you buy anything.

CREATE STORAGE

Consider multipurpose furnishings for your rooms that need storage.

- Wall-mounted media centers with closed-door cabinetry are great for all the electrical equipment no one wants to see.
- Large trunks or baskets with lids can serve double duty as a coffee table and storage for extra linens or toys.
- An armoire can serve as a mini home office in a dining room or bedroom.
- Most home stores now carry storage ottomans.
- Bookcases are great, but if you don't have anything attractive to display, consider bookcases with doors.
- Most home stores offer sliding, under-bed storage baskets. Because it can be a pain (literally) to get down on your knees all the time, only keep seldom-used items under your bed—like off-season clothes.

CHOOSE LIGHTING

Lighting choices fall into five categories:

- General lighting. This means regular overhead lights.
- Task lighting. These lights are mainly used to illuminate an area where you are working, reading, sewing, or cooking.
- Ambient lighting. This lighting creates very little shadow and washes the room with a glow. Think of crinkly Japanese lanterns or wall sconces.
- Accent lighting. This is directional lighting: table lamps, floor lamps, spotlights, up-lights, and the like.
- Utility lighting. This means floodlights and outdoor lighting.

Make the most of your lighting choices. Overhead lighting is too bright and shows every flaw in a room. Use dimmer switches in every room to hide your sins. Include a variety of fixtures at varying heights for more visual interest. Consider floor lamps, table lamps, spotlights on your wall art, recessed lighting in your bookcases and entertainment centers, and up-lights. An up-light placed behind a tree or large plant adds drama and will cast interesting shadows onto your ceiling through the leaves.

If you're trying to work with existing lamps but feel they are outdated, try a new lampshade. Most times, your lamp bases are fine; it's the dingy and dated lampshades that are making the fixtures look out of style. Visit your local lighting store to see the latest trends in lampshades.

FYI: Light fixtures come in many different finishes: silver, chrome, brass, black, and so on. Try to keep the finishes of your fixtures somewhat consistent throughout your home for a more elegant, put-together look.

ADD ARTWORK, ACCESSORIES, AND SMALL DETAILS

In my opinion, this is the area where most folks wander off track.

While the majority of people can handle buying a sofa, love seat, or bedroom set, the prospect of "filling in the rest" freaks them out. The difference between a well-appointed room and a junk shop is how you accessorize.

I've found that there are two types of accessorizers: the over-accessorizer and the under-accessorizer.

THE OVER-ACCESSORIZER

This person has no idea when to quit. If ever in doubt, she buys some more. Every horizontal surface in her home is covered with random crap that has no sense of restraint or cohesion.

YOU MAY BE AN OVER-ACCESSORIZER IF:

- ◉ You have more than four decorative pillows on your sofa.

- ◉ You have more than seven items on your mantel.

- ◉ You can't set a drink down on your nightstand.

- ◉ You have more than five pillows on your bed.

- ◉ You have an abundance of items that no one is allowed to use (e.g., fancy bath soaps, candles, hand towels, pillows, etc.).

- ◉ You have more than two "collections" of anything.

Don't overcrowd your home with collectibles. Each piece should have a purpose and/or meaning. It is so easy to get carried away. Shopping can be an emotional experience for many of us. You see something that makes your heart smile, and you impulsively throw down the credit card and take it home, with no idea what you're going to do with it. Resist the temptation to buy little knickknacks, pillows, throws, and paintings just because you like them. That is not reason enough. Each item you bring into your home should be special. It should have a purpose and a specific place in your home.

Editing is a very important component of design. Less is more, people.

THE UNDER-ACCESSORIZER

These folks are easy to spot; they don't do anything. You walk into their home and it looks like they haven't finished moving in yet. There may be one framed poster hung from a stray nail that was already there, but that's about it.

Identify the spaces you want to fill. Wall art usually should be in scale with the space it hangs in, which means you'll want large pieces for large spaces (over the sofa or mantel) and smaller pieces for smaller spaces (over doors or in between windows).

Balance is what's going to keep your décor from looking sporadic and lop-sided. Balanced arrangements can be either symmetrical or asymmetrical. Symmetrical arrangements are easier. It's a mirror image; items are perfectly equal on both sides of a center. Asymmetrical arrangements offer a quirkier, casual look, but they can be a bit harder to pull off. Get inspiration for composition from catalogs and magazines. Don't fixate on the exact items you see in the pages. Instead, study the shapes, scale, and color of the groupings. See if you can reproduce a similar arrangement with your own stuff.

Don't get wrapped up in everything being perfect. There's a principle in Japanese aesthetics called wabi-sabi. It's the concept of finding beauty and style in imperfection. Think about it: the world is imperfect, and it's divine still. Consider the uneven patina on aged copper or the random patterns on wood and granite. When you choose organic, asymmetrical arrangements, the imperfection seems natural.

ACCESSORIZING 101

- Create groupings. Combine objects with varying heights together in odd numbers. Three and five are good; any more is probably too much.

- Arrange similar items together according to color, shape, or design. A collection of vintage candlesticks has more impact when grouped together than when scattered throughout the house.

- Place mirrors so they reflect something pretty. Use them to add depth to a small space or reflect light in a dark room.

- Repeat a color at least three times in a room. If your area rug has a predominant color (say, red), consider including red candles on the mantel and a red accent pillow for the sofa.

- Instead of displaying your accessories in a straight line, create depth by zigzagging the pieces. Imagine a triangle, with the tallest pieces in the back.

- To avoid the blahs, combine items made from different textures. Position shiny finishes with matte ones or hard objects with softer ones. For example, if you have a grouping of chrome candlesticks with a glossy lacquer vase, be sure to include a rattan basket or live plant to soften the look.

- You should usually have a focal point. Arrange your smaller pieces around one major object to center the grouping. A large mirror over a fireplace mantel is a good example of a focal point.

ARTWORK

Impressive artwork doesn't have to be outrageously expensive. Consider some of these choices to cover your bare walls:

- Certain posters (framed nicely) are an inexpensive way to dress up a room. Browse online or at your local art museum store for suitable posters. Vintage or vintage reproduction is a good way to go here. You can find a nice variety on eBay.

- A collection of mixed vintage dishes displayed on a dining room wall adds a romantic, cottage feel to your home. Plain, white dishes hung on a darker wall create a more modern, graphic look.

- Take your own photos and frame them. You don't have to be a great photographer to make art. Go outside in the shade or on a cloudy day (bright sun can affect the quality of your photos) and take tight shots of flowers, clouds, treetops, siding on a home, fences, whatever strikes you. Get into Photoshop and crop the photos until they almost look abstract. Place your photos in matching frames, and display them in an attractive grouping on your wall.

- Vintage frames hung on a wall make a statement even without art inside. Find them on eBay or your local salvage yard. Paint them all the same color, and place them on your wall in a decorative manner. Think of the grouping as a single unit, a bit like a jigsaw puzzle. Test your arrangement on the floor first.

- Give old canvases a facelift with a coat of paint. You don't have to be an artist, just paint a few canvases the same color or paint each a coordinating color. Instant graphic art.

- Scour flea markets and online auctions for original art. There are scores of young artists out there and deals to be had.

- Wall decals have come a long way. On the Internet, you can find hundreds of stores selling very fun, hip decals for your walls. The advantage these decals have over wallpaper is they go up in minutes and most decals easily peel off with no damage to your wall. There's no commitment like with that pesky wallpaper.

- You can buy amazing original art for as cheap as $20/€15 at 20x200.com.

- Hanging art too high or too low. Make sure artwork is hung evenly throughout the room, with their vertical centers roughly at eye level. (Them's fightin' words for my husband and me. I'm 5 ft, 4 in/162 cm, and he's 6 ft, 2 in/188 cm. *Eye level* is a relative term.)

- Random placement. Display collections together for the biggest impact. A grouping of black-and-white photos in similar frames on one wall will make a stronger impact than various, mismatched frames all over the house. Try the arrangement out on the floor first before you start putting holes in the wall.

- Wrong scale and proportion. A general rule of thumb is that art pieces should not be larger than the piece of furniture below it. Otherwise, it can look top heavy.

INVESTMENT PIECES

As you've probably noted by now, I'm all for cutting corners. But there are certain items that I've found you really shouldn't skimp on. These invest-ment items will pay off in the long run.

Appliances, especially refrigerators » Older refrigerators are energy hogs and older washing machines waste water. Invest in Energy Star appliances. You will see the savings on your utility bill immediately.

Mattresses » This is how you rest, for chrissakes. A high-quality mattress may cost more up front (expect to pay $750 to $1,000/€525 to €700), but it will provide better support and should last up to 10 years if you flip it regularly.

Upholstery » Cheaply upholstered furniture is less durable and will need replacing more often than higher-quality pieces. Happily, most mid- to high-range furniture stores offer protection packages on construction and fabrics. This insurance policy will come in handy when kids and markers unite.

DO'S AND DON'TS FOR DANDY DÉCOR

DON'T follow the crowd. There's a verse in a Pete Seeger song (written by Malvina Reynolds; it's also the theme song to the show *Weeds*), "Little boxes on the hillside. Little boxes made of ticky-tacky, little boxes, little boxes, little boxes all the same." Embrace your individuality when nesting.

DON'T be too "crafty." Let's be honest: The crafts seldom look as good as in the magazines, faux-finishes are passé, hot glue doesn't hold, and papier-mâché is for preschoolers. Be creative, not crafty.

DO have a precise plan. See page 68.

DO bother to take measurements before you shop. It's hard to eyeball a room and get realistic measurements. God knows you don't want to drag a sofa back because it didn't fit. Take rough measurements and bring them with you when you shop.

DO take time when choosing paint colors. *Never* choose a paint color in the store. That fluorescent lighting makes everything look blue; impulsive buys will wreck your look. Also, NEVER, EVER buy that discounted "mistake" paint that the store has on sale. It's hard to make a color work just because it is inexpensive. There's usually a reason it's in the "mistake" pile, and it can be hard to match should you need more.

DON'T shove all your furniture up against the walls. I call this the dance floor syndrome. Unless you can rent the space out for raves on the weekends, pull your furnishings toward the center of the room for a more comfortable, inviting look.

DON'T assume that random purchases will just "fit in." I've heard this a million times from designers: "As long as you love all the pieces you buy, they will work together." That's a great place to start, but sometimes people take that as a license to run out and buy everything they love, which can be too much of a good thing. Less is more.

DO try and coordinate the colors and patterns in your room. There's a huge difference between "eclectic" and "erratic." Textile purchases shouldn't be matchy-matchy, but they should look like they know each other.

DON'T think that a simple table lamp or two is adequate lighting. I think lighting is about 75 percent of good design. You miss out on a lot of visual interest by not using a variety of options. (See what your options are on page 84.)

DO "edit" your rooms. Design is usually much more about what you remove from the space, not what you add.

DON'T worry about what other people are going to think. Just because your home doesn't look like the cover of *Architectural Digest* doesn't mean it isn't fabulous. Enjoy your home.

WHEN TO HIRE A PROFESSIONAL

Face it, you can't do everything yourself. Sometimes you gotta call in a pro. Here is a list of professionals who can help you keep your home stylish and safe.

HOUSEKEEPING

The perfect scenario would be to have a housekeeper come in every other week. That way all you have to do is "straighten" in between cleanings. Someday, when I win the lottery, I'm going to do that. In the meantime, I suggest getting a crew in at least every season. It's a real treat, and you deserve it.

How to Hire a Housekeeper

The best way to find a housekeeper is to ask your friends for recommendations. If that doesn't work, consider a housekeeping service. The major advantage of working with an agency is that it has dozens of employees. You can test-drive its cleaners one at a time, until you find the right one. If you're unhappy with the service, it's not like you have to fire anybody face-to-face; all you have to do is tell the agency to send somebody new. Make sure the agency is bonded and insured, just in case.

FYI: Pay by the hour, instead of a flat rate. This will ensure a more thorough job.

It may seem obvious, but don't leave valuables out, and be clear with the housekeeper so there are no misunderstandings about responsibilities and payment structure.

PEST CONTROL

Over-the-counter pesticides can be harmful to children, pets, you, and the environment, and they usually don't even work. Don't run out and buy random poisons that could hurt you and your family. The best attack is defense. Bugs come indoors for food and water. Make sure all the food items in your pantry are sealed tight. Check your houseplants. Are you overwatering them? The stagnant water that collects in the saucers are perfect watering holes for ants and cockroaches. If you've tried all this and you've still got bugs, it's time to call a professional. Visit www.callyourpro.com for FAQs and contact information for professionals in your area who use environmentally smart options for pest control.

INTERIOR DESIGNER

If you've used all of my fabulous decorating tricks, but you still feel like you're not getting it right, you may consider hiring an interior designer. The very thought of hiring a professional designer can give you hives, I understand. It can be hard to figure out how they charge and what you're getting for your money. Like hiring a housekeeper, references from friends will save you a lot of time and money in finding the right person. If none of your friends can help, visit the American Society of Interior Designers Web site (www.asid.org) for FAQs and references.

You'll want to set up an initial consultation with the designer at your home. This is when you get to know each other and discuss the project. Ask to see a portfolio of the designer's previous projects. Some designers will come to your home free of charge, but frankly, you get what you pay for here. Expect to pay an agreed-on hourly rate plus travel time.

THE MANY MYSTERIOUS WAYS DESIGNERS CHARGE FOR THEIR SERVICES

Retainers ⋈ Once an agreement has been reached, an interior designer might request a retainer fee in advance. This fee covers the planning process and is usually applied to the cost of the project.

Flat fee ⋈ In this case, the designer will review and evaluate the entire scope of your project. A bid is submitted, and the fee is paid in increments throughout the process. The fee schedule will depend on when items are received and delivered or subcontractor services are rendered. Once again, you get what you pay for here, so don't jump on the cheapest bid.

FYI: Keep in mind that a bid is a lot like an estimate. It can get out of hand if you don't stay on top of the expenses.

Cost, plus » This is sort of like working on commission. The designer "marks up" all the items purchased and keeps the difference. I'm sure most designers are extremely ethical, but be warned that this is a situation where they can "getcha." Designers often receive a designer's discount or wholesale price at many retail outlets. They may not tell you this. They *may* tell you they are paying full price for these items and then mark the merchandise up accordingly. I have seen this happen. Be sure to inquire about any discounts they will receive and take long, hard looks at the receipts to ensure you're not paying too much for the services rendered.

Retail » Many furniture stores offer free design services with the purchase of their products. Between you and me, I don't think this is the best way to hire design services. The designers are also the salespeople, who may or may not have any design experience and are working on *commission*. Motivations for the sale may vary depending on which salesperson you get. Also, unlike more traditional interior design services, these folks can only work with the products they sell in their store. This can be very limiting when building a decorating plan.

Hourly » This is the best option for smaller jobs. If you are simply having trouble pulling your look together, hire a designer by the hour. She can give you ideas, which you can then implement (saving you tons of money). Fees range from around $75 to $250/€50 to €175 per hour, depending on the level of expertise and area of the country.

N ow that you've learned practically all there is to know about slacker chic, I want to share with you some of my favorite tips and tricks to get it.

eBay ❧ Type *anything* into the search bar, and you will find it. Done right, you can get amazing deals. I've purchased vintage Guatemalan santos, full sets of antique transferware, architectural salvage, original art, and the most unique small furnishings and accessories you've ever seen—all for pennies on the dollar. It's like an online flea market.

Etsy.com ❧ The same as eBay, but the merchandise is all handmade crafts. This site is full of vendors who actually have the time to craft beautiful items that they sell on the site. Get the look of handcrafted, without the actual handcrafting.

Fan decks from the paint store ❧ Not just for choosing paint colors, these decks (purchased at any paint store for around $20/€15) can act as a color reference guide for all of your design projects.

An old dresser ❧ Forget an expensive closet system. If you have a short dresser, slide it into your closet. You'll find it perfect for little things like socks, T-shirts, ties and scarves, and kids' clothes. Paint it the same color as the closet wall, and suddenly it's a custom closet.

Clippy rings ❧ These are great. You can find clippy rings wherever window treatments are sold. They make it possible to hang just about anything from a curtain rod. Secure a rod to a wall and hang saris, quilts, fabric by the yard, or even rugs for a new take on wall art.

Hem tape » Never sew again. Adhesive hem tape is sold in rolls at fabric stores. Iron it on to whatever you are hemming. You can also use hem tape to apply ribbon and decorative trim to curtain panels and to hem your kid's pants.

Live plants instead of cut flowers » Cut flowers are expensive and then you just have to sit and watch them die. Potted plants are a bigger bang for your buck. (See which plants are the hardest to kill on page 98.)

Overhead projectors » You can make hand-painted wall murals quickly and easily with the help of an overhead projector. You can usually rent projectors at the library, but you can also buy them at art supply stores for around $60/€40. Pull graphic clip art images from the Internet—the less detail, the better. Place the image in the projector, and trace on your wall. Then color between the lines with a small, high-quality paintbrush. I've painted words, flowers, cacti, and abstract art. The finished product can be spectacular, and the process could not be easier.

Casters and screw-on legs » Turn just about anything into a coffee table by attaching wheels or legs. Casters and screw-on legs can be found at any hardware store.

Specialty paper » Wrapping paper has come a long way, baby. Peruse your local specialty paper store for inexpensive and easy artwork. Just place the paper in the right frame, with the right mat.

Duct tape »

- Removes lint from upholstery.

- Catches flies.

- Keeps picture frames even. Do your framed art pieces become crooked over time? This can wreck the look of a gallery wall. Loop a small piece of duct tape, and place it behind the frame. It will secure the piece to the wall—no slipping.

- Replaces a torn shower curtain grommet. This looks best when used on the liner, not the actual shower curtain that people can see.

- Repairs a vacuum cleaner hose.

- Hangs Christmas lights without putting nail holes in the house.

- Repairs a photo frame. Sometimes those little "legs" that hold the frame upright fall off. Duct tape saves the day.

- Keeps small accessories steady on bookshelves. I live in earthquake country, so all my little treasures are duct-taped down. Loop the duct tape, and tuck it under the items so it doesn't show.

Aluminum foil ✂ Wrap foil around hinges and hardware when painting doors to keep them drip free.

HOW TO FAKE A GREEN THUMB

*I used to kill every plant I brought into the house. Every single one. My hus-
band would whistle the "Funeral March" every time I introduced a new piece
of helpless greenery into our home.*

*Finally, I'd had enough. I decided to start over. I educated myself
about plants that were harder to kill and filled in with artificial. Fake
plants get a really bad rap. Everyone immediately thinks of those hideous
silk pothos and ivy you see at the craft store. (Honestly, it would look
more realistic if you just put some bubble wrap in a clay pot.) As a general rule, I find that the grassy plants made from rubber look much more
realistic than the silk ones that look like leaves. If you mix a few fakes with
a few hard-to-kill live plants, it will appear that they are all real.*

**PLANTS THAT REQUIRE LITTLE CARE OR DIRECT
SUNLIGHT:**

 Ivy ❧ The most common ivy houseplants have leaves that look
like birds' feet. Don't overwater an ivy, and let it thrive in a shady
corner of your home.

 Peace lily ❧ This plant has large, glossy leaves that will droop
when it needs watering. It has pretty, white flowers that bloom
throughout the year and thrives in low light.

 Philodendron ❧ There are many different species of philodendrons,
with many varieties of leaf size, shape, and coloring. Some species
climb like ivy, while others are shaped more like shrubs. What they
all have in common is their ability to survive neglect. Keep them in
medium, filtered light, and water them when they look droopy.

Dragon tree ⚘ This plant has several spindly "trunks" with narrow, spiky leaves. Very "Dr. Seuss," they look great in a modern, minimalist setting. Yellowing leaves can be an indication of overwatering. If you don't water enough, the leaves will start to droop.

 Airplane or spider plant ⚘ A little water, a little sun, and spider plants usually stay lush and healthy. They're also easy to reproduce: Pick the "baby spiders" off the stems, and simply plant in a pot.

 Wax plant ⚘ Just like ivies and spider plants, wax plants are hardy hanging plants. Although they will need a little more direct sunlight than the ivy and spider plants, curtain-filtered sunlight should be just fine.

 Snake plant or mother-in-law's tongue ⚘ Snake plants can take as much or as little sun as you give them; they are notoriously hardy and hard to kill. This houseplant has stiff, upright leaves and can grow to as much as 4 ft/12 cm tall. (I actually did kill one once, but I didn't notice for more than a year. The leaves remained upright and green posthumously.)

PLANTS THAT REQUIRE LITTLE CARE AND LOTS OF SUN:

 Cacti ⚘ Tall, thorny cacti make wonderful architectural statements in a room, but if you have kids, they can be hazardous. Bishop's Cap and Christmas cactus are not thorny but equally hardy.

 Aloe and succulents ⚘ While these plants can take the heat, avoid direct, scorching sun. A medicinal plant, aloe can be used to treat minor burns. Simply break off a leaf, and squeeze the gel onto the burn.

 Bromeliads ⚘ Bromeliads love the sun and typically grow in a rosette form with a center "well." To water, simply fill the well. These plants need to be in warm rooms. They are tropical plants and can die when chilled.

THE HALF-ASSED
HOSTESS

I'm not concerned with proper table settings, seating arrangements, or formal etiquette. Who can have a good time with all those rules? How can you enjoy yourself if you're worried whether you're using the right fork or wondering whether the pumpkin is the bowl or part of the meal?

—AMY SEDARIS, *I LIKE YOU*

E ntertaining is supposed to be fun, for you and your guests. Spending all day cleaning and all night prepping, plating, serving, and washing up is not my idea of a good time. Well, not anymore.

I used to throw these crazy Día de los Muertos parties every year. It was what I lived for. Very much like Burning Man or maybe even the Olympics, preparations began far in advance, the budget could support a small developing nation, and I was a total mess the whole time. It took a fairly serious party injury for me to realize that maybe I was in over my head.

THE PARTY THAT ALMOST KILLED ME

The day of my annual Día de los Muertos party had finally arrived. One hundred eighty-five of our closest friends would be showing up at our doorstep any minute. As usual, I was dead set and determined to make sure every last one of them would be thoroughly impressed and amazed by my household superiority.

I'd spent weeks poring over every detail, and it was finally coming together. Freshly squeezed lime juice and crushed mint for the mojitos? Check. Authentic Oaxacan festival masks hung on the foyer staircase with care? Check. Homicidal threats made to any child who might decide to trash their room? Check.

Candles flickered from every surface, the aroma of sliced mango and toasting tortillas filled the space, and I'd finally finished the pièce de résistance: a handmade Day of the Dead altar, consisting of family photographs and hand-illustrated memorials hung by ribbons from painted tree branches. All of this I placed on the foyer table in a beautiful crystal vase we got as a wedding gift. As I gazed up at my magnificent creation, I said a little prayer, a prayer for anyone who might be foolish enough to *even think* about touching it.

As I glanced at my reflection just moments before the first guests were to arrive, I noticed a tiny smudge at the very top of the bathroom mirror. Initially, I tried to ignore it, but it eventually wore me down. "Martha would never host a party with a huge smudge like that on her mirror," echoed through my head. So, I gingerly scaled the bathroom countertop, in my heels, and stood on stretched tiptoe to remove the offending smudge. That's when I slipped. My big toe broke the fall by breaking itself. It was at that very moment, as I lay on the floor, crying in pain, that I looked up and saw that I'd only made the smudge worse . . . and did I smell *something burning*?

Yes, something was burning, but that was the least of my problems. My toe swelled up like a baby eggplant, and I ended up hobbling around in Crocs all night like an idiot. I couldn't wear proper shoes for six months. I have not thrown a huge party since, and I gotta tell you, I don't miss it one bit. Parties are supposed to be fun, not excruciating.

. . .

Love to entertain, but not sure why sometimes? It's easy to get lost in the minutiae of "event planning" and forget why you're entertaining in the first place. When a hostess is so wrapped up in the details that she misses out on the conversation, she's also missing the point. Forget the formalities. Be a half-assed hostess. Do what you like to do, and cheat the rest.

In this section, I will share some of my tips for entertaining. Whether it's dinner for the kids, parties for the adults, or accommodating out-of-towners, I've got you covered.

We'll start with the family and kid-related stuff and then move on to the more adult-themed entertaining. (I swear I'm not talking about orgies. Please read on.) To round it all out, I've also included some guidance on how to host houseguests without wanting to poison them by the end of the week.

EASY ENTERTAINING? YEAH, RIGHT.

One evening not too long ago, I was in a long line at the grocery store with my kids. My little ones were experiencing a low-blood-sugar crash: intermittently poking each other, tattling, and begging me for M&M's. As most moms would do in this situation, I was hiding out in my "happy place."

In my haze, I happened to glance down at a certain cooking magazine. The headline was "Easy Entertaining!" The accompanying photo was of a small tea sandwich. The tiny treat consisted of repeating layers of bread, smoked salmon, cucumber, marinated red onion, fresh dill, and aioli. Each tidbit was cut into a cute little triangle shape, with the crusts removed. The cucumber had obviously been run through one of those Salamander slicers, because it had an adorable little zigzag shape along its edges. There was a fancy toothpick involved. I gasped at the audacity.

That is not easy entertaining, people. That is slightly less complicated entertaining than perhaps a White House dinner. Seriously, how can you call that sandwich "easy" with a straight face? You'd have to make at least fifty of them to feed a party of four.

Let me tell you what's easy: ordering a pizza and popping a beer. That's easy entertaining.

KITCHEN STAPLES FOR THE HALF-ASSED HOSTESS

The half-assed hostess has no time (or desire) to plan exquisite meals. Usually she is rushing in from work, greeted at the door by two kids. One is crying; the other doesn't know where her homework is—and it's due tomorrow.

When entertaining on a larger scale, it can be just as hard to pull together the perfect, easy party tray. I consulted my friend Mike Zimmerman, celebrated San Francisco chef and television personality, about a pantry list for the half-assed hostess. I wanted to find out what we need in our kitchens to pull together quick, easy, and delicious meals for family and entertaining. He helped me come up with the following lists.

PANTRY STAPLES

- assorted nuts
- black beans
- bread crumbs (regular and panko)
- caviar (don't forget the wasabi type—great color, great garnish)
- chicken broth
- chickpeas
- cornmeal
- crackers
- dried fruit
- dried pasta
- garlic
- marinara sauce
- olives
- onions

- pita bread
- popcorn (make flavored corn for snacks)
- potatoes
- refried beans
- rice
- roasted red peppers (you can get these in a jar in the gourmet section of your grocery store)
- water chestnuts (sauté with bacon, chop, and place in wonton wrappers for the best wontons ever)

BAKING STAPLES

- all-purpose/plain flour
- brown sugar
- cornstarch/corn flour
- granulated sugar
- real vanilla extract/essence

CONDIMENTS

- balsamic vinegar
- barbecue sauce
- canned tomatoes with chiles
- capers
- evaporated milk (to thicken soups or sauces)
- extra-virgin olive oil
- honey
- jams (to make sweet desserts and savory glazes for chicken, fish, etc.)
- ketchup
- maple syrup (makes a delicious glaze for duck and ham)
- mustards (yellow, Dijon)
- peanut/groundnut butter (not just for sandwiches—quick sate sauce for skewers or noodle salad)

- red wine vinegar
- salsa
- soy sauce
- tahini (to make any type of bean into a hummus or spread)
- tapenades
- Thai chile aioli (this condiment can be found at any Asian market and is the perfect dipping sauce for those little frozen appetizers you can get at the grocery)
- tubes of sun-dried tomato paste, minced garlic, and chopped black olive paste
- vegetable oil (when you don't want to taste the oil and for frying)
- Vietnamese garlic-chile paste
- Worcestershire sauce

FRIDGE STAPLES

- apples (sliced baked apples on puff pastry make a quick tart)
- cheeses
- cream cheese
- ginger (can even be frozen and used as needed)
- half-and-half/half cream
- horseradish
- hummus
- lemons
- limes
- olives from an olive bar (kalamata, niçoise, etc.)
- polenta (buy this premade in a tube)
- simple syrup (make it yourself, it's just equal parts water and sugar melted into a syrup on the stove, and keep on hand—lasts forever; good for bar and beverages)
- sour cream
- tortillas (corn and flour)

- wonton wrappers (you've got enough ingredients here to make any number of wontons and sauces or quick ravioli or even desserts)

FREEZER STAPLES

- bacon
- butter (won't go rancid in the freezer)
- chicken breasts (for skewers, etc.)
- ground turkey
- petite peas
- phyllo dough (for tarts, strudels)
- puff pastry (to make pizza, sausage rolls, and desserts— tarts, napoleons, etc.)
- pumpkin seeds, pine nuts (to make quick pestos— they won't go rancid in the freezer)
- sausages
- shrimp/prawns

HERBS AND SPICES

- allspice
- arrowroot
- basil
- bay leaves
- cayenne pepper
- celery seed
- chile powder
- cinnamon (ground is fine)
- cloves
- coriander, ground
- cumin, ground
- curry powder
- dill

- fennel seeds
- garlic powder
- ginger
- marjoram
- nutmeg
- onion flakes
- oregano
- paprika
- peppercorns
- red pepper flakes
- rosemary
- sage
- salt (I like to have sea salt and kosher)
- sesame seeds
- tarragon
- thyme

Fresh herbs are always better than dried; it's a fact. Not only do they taste better, but arranged on top of a half-assed meal, fresh herbs give the illusion that you really cooked something. What people might not know is how easy they are to grow. Use a couple large strawberry pots to plant rosemary, sage, basil, dill, mint, nasturtiums, thyme, and marjoram. Put them in a sunny spot and water them occasionally. I have a large terra-cotta pot on my patio that contains a small lemon tree, rosemary, thyme, oregano, and basil. This one pot contains almost every flavoring I use. Plant a pot today to make all your half-assed recipes look and taste better. If you don't have the space or time to plant, most stores sell fresh herbs washed and ready to go. You can also buy all of these herbs dried. Keep them in a dark pantry. Sunlight may cause jarred herbs and spices to lose their flavor.

FYI: Mike suggests you cook with kosher salt and then finish food with sea salt or other high-end salts. He also recommends getting a small coffee grinder and designating it for spices. That way you can buy your spices whole and use them either whole or ground. (I personally find that last piece of advice far too professional for my half-assed hostessing, but there you go.)

- apricot brandy
- cocktail onions
- coffee
- Cointreau
- cola (regular and diet)
- cranberry juice
- gin
- lemon-lime soda
- limoncello
- olives
- red wine
- rum
- sake
- soda water
- teas
- tequila
- tonic water
- vermouth
- vodka
- whiskey
- white wine

- bottle opener
- corkscrew
- muddler
- shaker
- strainer

SOME TOOLS

- assorted baking pans/tins (8-by-8-in/20-by-20-cm square, 8-in/20-cm round, 9-by-13-in/23-by-33-cm rectangular, loaf pan/tin, etc.)
- baking sheets/trays
- muffin tins (regular and mini)
- skewers
- toothpicks

SERVING STAPLES

- all-white dishware—platters, plates, and bowls. It's just easier to use all white. (You can get fabulous and frugal white dishware at IKEA.) Dress up your tablescape with flowers or seasonal/holiday items like chargers, table runners, napkins, and candles (tea, votive, pillar, and column).
- chopsticks
- cocktail napkins—lots!
- fresh leaves from your garden (make sure they're not poisonous!) instead of doilies. Try hydrangea, ivy, fig leaves, etc.
- silverware
- small shot glasses (for soup shots, creamy dessert bites)
- squeeze bottles (to do creams and sauces—gives a professional look in no time at all)
- take-out containers

I'm all about quick and easy family meals. And what's quicker and easier than chicken? But let's face it—raw chicken is gross. It's so full of germs that you're supposed to use separate cutting boards, knives, and dishcloths, and you need to wash your hands every five minutes. Once you're done, you have to disinfect like you're cleaning an operating room. We half-assed hostesses can't take that kind of pressure. A preroasted chicken from the supermarket deli costs around $7/€5, can be picked up on the way home, and can feed a family of four. At the end of the day, if I haven't prepared for dinner (which is almost every night), I'll run to the store and grab one of these little delicacies. If my pantry is stocked with the right essentials (see page 104), the chicken is all I need to buy.

I will warn you, I am NOT a chef, and I'm not much for real recipes. I'm just a mom trying to get dinner on the table—my standards are fairly low. I rarely measure anything, and I implore you to do the same. In fact, I haven't even included measurements in most of the following recipes. Feel free to play around with these ideas. I'm sure you can come up with even better ones if you put your mind to it. Most of these recipes involve ripping the meat into shreds. If you have super-picky kids like mine, consider chopping off the wings and legs for them before you get started. That way the kids can have something "plainer," and you don't have to make an entirely different meal for them.

CHICKEN PARMESAN

I prefer to bake this dish without the bread coating. It's not like my recipe is incredibly dietetic, but I figure every calorie counts.

deli chicken
cooking spray
jarred marinara or pasta sauce of your choice
shredded mozzarella
pasta of your choice (I like thin spaghetti), cooked

To prepare, shred the chicken into pieces. Coat a baking sheet/tray with cooking spray, and arrange serving-size portions of chicken in piles. Pour some marinara sauce over the chicken, and top with the mozzarella. Pop it under the broiler until the cheese melts. Pick up with a spatula and place over the pasta, then eat.

CHICKEN AND DUMPLINGS

deli chicken
8 cups/2 L low-sodium chicken broth
1 medium onion, peeled
fresh sage
fresh thyme
fresh marjoram
kitchen twine
1 can buttermilk biscuits

To prepare, shred the chicken into bite-size portions. Pour the broth into a large pot. Add the chicken, onion (whole), and herbs. I find that if you tie the herbs together tightly with the twine, you have fewer bits and pieces floating around in your stew. Simmer on medium-high heat until it starts to boil. Cut each biscuit into quarters, and drop the pieces into the pot. When the dumplings get all poofy, it's done. Remove the onion and herbs, and serve. For a lower-calorie "dumpling," substitute the biscuits with flour tortillas. If you prefer chicken noodle soup, replace the biscuits with egg noodles. Just make sure to cook the noodles in water before adding them to the pot. You can also add some frozen peas and carrots.

CHICKEN TOSTADAS

deli chicken
refried beans
black beans
butter
flour or corn tortillas
sour cream
1 avocado, sliced
shredded cheese
lettuce
1 medium onion, finely chopped
salsa

To prepare, shred the chicken and set it aside. Mix together the refried and black beans. Heat them in the microwave. Melt a pat of butter in a frying pan. Place one tortilla in the butter and cook until crispy on both sides. Assemble by spreading the bean mixture on a tortilla, followed by the shredded chicken. Add the other ingredients to taste.

CHICKEN TERIYAKI

Steamed snow peas are good to throw in with this dish.

deli chicken
teriyaki sauce (you can make your own by combining soy sauce
    and brown sugar over low heat)
brown or white rice, cooked

To prepare, shred the chicken, and sauté with the teriyaki sauce in a pan.
Serve over the rice.

WAYNE'S DELI-LICIOUS CHICKEN SALAD

The chicken salad is better if you let it sit in the fridge overnight.

deli chicken
1 red onion
2 Fuji apples
green grapes
red grapes
handful of chopped pecans
mayonnaise
ground black pepper
baguette

To prepare, shred the chicken and place in a large mixing bowl. Chop the
onion, apples, and grapes into small pieces and throw in the bowl. Add the
pecans, moisten with the mayonnaise, season with pepper, and stir with
a large spoon. Everything is to taste, so just figure it out. Serve on slices
of baguette.

CHICKEN PICCATA

deli chicken
$^1/_4$ cup/30 g all-purpose/plain flour
3 lemons
garlic powder
about 1 tbsp/15 ml olive oil
$^1/_3$ cup/75 ml dry white wine
low-sodium chicken broth
1 small jar artichoke hearts
capers
linguine or spaghetti, cooked
salt and ground black pepper

To prepare, shred the chicken and set aside. Combine the flour, the zest of 1 lemon, and the garlic powder; mix well. Add the chicken and turn to coat. Shake off excess flour. Heat the olive oil in a large skillet over medium-high heat. Add chicken and sauté for 2 minutes per side, until golden brown and cooked through. Add the juice of 2 lemons, the wine, and broth and bring to a simmer. Simmer for 5 minutes, until the sauce thickens. Add the artichoke hearts and capers, and simmer for 1 minute to heat through. Serve over linguine. Season with salt and pepper.

CHICKEN CAESAR SALAD

deli chicken
1 bag Caesar salad

To prepare, shred the chicken and toss with the bag of Caesar salad. The dressing and croutons come in the bag. Voilà!

THAI CHICKEN

deli chicken

about 8 tbsp peanut/groundnut butter (chunky or creamy)

about ½ cup/120 ml water

a few dashes soy sauce

about 1 tbsp/15 g brown sugar

garlic (fresh is better, but powder is fine)

crushed red pepper flakes

1 bag veggies (you can find this near the bagged salad at your grocery store)

splash of peanut/groundnut or canola oil

To prepare, shred the chicken and mix it with all the other ingredients, except the oil. Heat the oil over high heat in a nonstick wok or sauté pan. Add mixture and cook until the peanut sauce is smooth. This should take no more than a few minutes.

MONTEREY CHICKEN

This is great served with a baked potato (okay, microwaved potato) and a small salad.

deli chicken

cooking spray

barbecue sauce

precooked bacon (you can find it with the regular bacon)

shredded cheese

To prepare, shred the chicken into pieces. Coat a baking sheet/tray with cooking spray and arrange serving-size portions of chicken in piles. Pour a little barbecue sauce onto each pile. Place two pieces of bacon over the chicken, and sprinkle cheese over the top. Pop under the broiler until the cheese melts.

CHICKEN FAJITAS

deli chicken

1 onion

1 bell pepper/capsicum

olive oil

refried beans

flour tortillas

sour cream

avocado slices

shredded cheese

salsa

To prepare, shred the chicken and dice the onion and bell pepper/ capsicum. Using a nonstick pan, sauté all three ingredients in a small amount of oil until the onion and bell pepper/capsicum are tender. Heat the beans and tortillas in the microwave. Build the fajitas any way your family likes with the rest of the ingredients, and serve it up!

CHICKEN ENCHILADAS

deli chicken

1 can enchilada sauce

corn tortillas

1 small onion, chopped

shredded cheese

To prepare, shred the chicken and set aside. Coat the bottom of a glass baking dish with the enchilada sauce. Wrap small portions of the shredded chicken in the tortillas. Place the stuffed tortillas in the pan, and cover with more enchilada sauce, the onion, and cheese. Bake at 350°F/180°C/gas 4 until heated all the way through—usually around 20 minutes.

CHINESE CHICKEN WRAPS

deli chicken
1 bag Chinese chicken salad
flour tortillas

To prepare, shred the chicken and mix with all the ingredients that come in a Chinese chicken salad bag. Fold portions into flour tortillas and eat.

CHICKEN ALFREDO

deli chicken
$^1/_2$ cup/115 g unsalted butter
8 oz/225 g cream cheese
garlic powder
about 2 cups/480 ml milk
about $^1/_2$ cup/60 g shredded Parmesan cheese
ground black pepper
cooked pasta

To prepare, shred the chicken and set aside. Melt the butter in a medium, nonstick saucepan over medium heat. Add the cream cheese and garlic powder, stirring with a wire whisk until smooth. Add the milk, a little at a time, whisking to smooth out lumps. Stir in the Parmesan and season with pepper. Remove from the heat when the sauce reaches the desired consistency. The sauce will thicken rapidly; thin with milk if cooked too long. Toss the sauce with the chicken and hot pasta to serve. If you want to slack off even more, just buy a package of Alfredo mix in lieu of the sauce recipe above. You can find the packets in the spice aisle of your supermarket.

BARBECUE CHICKEN PIZZA

This is a half-assed homage to the famous California Pizza Kitchen BBQ Chicken Pizza.

deli chicken

barbecue sauce (honey flavor is best for this recipe)

Boboli pizza crust

shredded cheese (a mix of mozzarella and Monterey Jack is nice)

1 red onion, chopped

cilantro

To prepare, shred the chicken and mix with a small amount of the barbecue sauce (just to coat). Spread a nice coating of barbecue sauce on the pizza crust. Sprinkle a healthy amount of cheese all over the top, then add your chicken, onion, and cilantro. Bake at 350°F/180°C/gas 4 until the cheese is all melty and the crust is toasty brown.

SPICY JAMBALAYA

deli chicken

2 packages dry jambalaya mix (usually found near the rice and
    dried beans at the supermarket)

8 oz/225 g kielbasa or smoked sausage, sliced

green/spring onions, chopped

To prepare, shred the chicken and set aside. Follow the directions on the jambalaya mix, and add the shredded chicken and sausage. Sprinkle green/spring onions on top for the last step. *AIEEE!!*

SAVORY SMOTHERED CHICKEN AND BISCUITS

deli chicken

1 small package frozen peas

1 can cream of chicken soup

$^{1}/_{2}$ cup/120 ml low-fat sour cream

$^{1}/_{2}$ cup/120 ml milk

salt and ground black pepper

$^{1}/_{2}$ cup/60 g shredded cheese

1 can flour biscuits (savory)

To prepare, shred the chicken and place in a saucepan with the peas, soup, sour cream, and milk. Season with salt and pepper. Once it's boiling, pour the mixture into a glass baking dish, and sprinkle the cheese over it. Bake at 400°F/200°C/gas 6 for 15 to 20 minutes. Cook the biscuits according to the instructions on the package. Pour the chicken mixture over the biscuits and you're done.

AUNT MEL'S FAMOUS CHICKEN AND GREEN CHILE CASSEROLE

deli chicken

1 medium onion, coarsely chopped

olive oil

3 tbsp/45 g all-purpose/plain flour

1 cup/240 ml milk

1 cup/240 ml low-sodium chicken broth

1 small jar chopped green chiles

1 can Rotel (diced tomato and green chile)

10 to 12 flour tortillas, cut or torn into bite-size bits

about 1 lb/455 g shredded cheddar cheese

To prepare, shred the chicken and set aside. Sauté the onion using a splash of olive oil for about 1 minute. Add the flour and stir until the onion is coated. Add the milk and broth; stir until the sauce thickens. Mix in the green chiles and Rotel. Place a layer of shredded chicken in a casserole dish. Next, layer with the tortilla bits, cheese, and the sauce. Repeat with cheese on top. This is a great dish to double up on—make two and freeze the other.

REALITY CHECK ON KIDS' PARTIES

Before we move on to adult entertaining, let's spend a moment on kids' parties because they've gotten completely out of control. When I was growing up, my dad often muttered under his breath, "The more you do for them, the less they appreciate it." Kids' parties these days are the perfect example of that. I swear to you, I have attended parties for *four-year-olds* that cost more than my wedding: ponies, clowns, rock-climbing walls, magicians, jumpy castles, videographers, and goodie bags like the ones they give out at the Oscars. (That kid is *totally* going to expect a ride on the space shuttle next year.) These over-the-top parties aren't good for anyone. Take it down a notch, kids just want the cake and the present; they really don't care about much else. Make it easy on yourself. If you're having the party at your house, keep it simple. If you want even less work, consider taking the kids *somewhere else* (where they pay people to set up and clean up).

EASY ACTIVITIES

I've compiled a list of fun activities that don't take a ton of preparation or money. These are also wonderful games for independent play or even playdates.

Dress up ✎ This is great if you've got a load of clothes that you can't seem to get over to Goodwill. Pull them out and let the kids go to town. Have a runway show and take photos.

Red carpet ✎ Have the kids come in dress-up clothes. Take photos of them as they enter, like paparazzi. Serve popcorn and candy on TV trays, and let them watch a movie (or two).

Camping party ✎ Put up a tent in the backyard, and serve hot dogs and s'mores. Tell a scary story, then wait to see how long it takes them to run back into the house.

Collage ✎ Have the kids cut out and glue images from old magazines onto a box or sheet of paper.

Scribble game ✎ My kids LOVE this game, and it's a fun and easy way to spark creativity. One person scribbles onto a piece of drawing paper (let's say, a zigzag shape). The other person must transform the scribble into a recognizable drawing. In this case, the zigzag could be transformed into spikes on a *T. rex* or a line of rooftops.

Chalk art ✎ Keep this activity outside. Chalk dust is a pain to clean out of your home. Get the big sidewalk chalk, and play four square, tic-tac-toe, or hopscotch.

Post office ✎ This can be fun for smaller kids. Use your junk mail and have the kids put stickers on the envelopes as stamps. Cut a slot out of an old box, and use that as the mailbox.

SpongeBob's adventure ✎ This is another fun outdoor activity that is super-easy. Fill two buckets with water and place them about 4 ft/122 cm apart. Have the kids dunk a rectangular yellow sponge (SpongeBob) into the water and then toss it to the other child. Then the other child gets a turn. This is great for a hot day.

Make hats ⚮ Create fancy hats out of paper plates, construction paper, and any fabric or paper scraps you have lying around. Use the bows and ribbon from the gifts.

Puzzles ⚮ Mix up the pieces and let them have at it.

Build a town ⚮ Cut the bottoms off milk cartons and make different-sized buildings. Cover the cartons with brown craft paper, and have the kids draw the windows and other architectural details.

Doll clothing ⚮ Barbie fashions are always more fun when they're home-made. Provide the kids with felt, kid scissors, tape, and pipe cleaners.

Cereal necklaces ⚮ Kids love this project. Just provide some yarn and Froot Loops or Cheerios. The kids can make patterns with the colors.

Homemade Play-Doh ⚮ Fun to make and fun to play with.

> 1 cup/200 g salt
> 1/2 cup/60 g cornstarch/corn flour
> 3/4 cup/180 ml water
> food coloring (this is totally optional,
>   and frankly I prefer not to use it—it stains)

Combine the salt and cornstarch/corn flour in a large bowl. Make a well in the mixture. Add the water and food coloring (if using), and knead until smooth. Store in an airtight container.

Board games ⚮ You got 'em, they play 'em.

Hula hoop ⚮ This is a good core workout for Mom.

Fort ⚮ If you have boxes left over from a move, great, but you can also use a blanket and cushions from the sofa.

Mani/pedi sleepover » Little girls love fingernail polish. Tell all the girls to bring their robes. You can put their hair up in towels, paint their nails, and send them off to watch a princess DVD.

Tattoo parlor » Temporary tattoos are cheap, and kids love them.

Peanut dolls » All you need are some whole peanuts in the shell and some pipe cleaners. Cut four small holes in the peanut shell, and run two pieces of pipe cleaner through the peanut for arms and legs. Have the kids draw little faces and hair on the shells. You can make a peanut-family house out of a shoebox.

Make your own food » You want to go with food that can be assembled. Pizza and sundaes are just right for this party. Lay a cheap plastic tarp in the backyard or over your kitchen table, and let them go at it.

Run through the sprinkler » No explanation necessary, really.

Mud pies » An oldie but goodie. Save the tins from potpies. Kids can use leaves, rocks, or whatever they find for decoration.

Fear factor » This theme is very similar to the old Halloween parties where you'd put your hands in a box full of gross stuff. Spaghetti = worms, peeled grapes = eyeballs, etc. Have them bob for gummy worms floating in fruit punch or strawberry soda—it looks like blood. On the Internet, you can buy gelatin molds that look like brains.

Go out » Take the kids to the zoo, a children's/science museum, an arcade, or a pizza parlor.

Junior Olympics » Have the kids participate in athletic competitions in the backyard: potato sack races, the old "balloon between the knees" race, an obstacle course made from whatever you can find in the garage, and gymnastics (frontward rolls are fine). You can buy cheap gold medals at any party store. Make sure you get enough for everybody.

KIDS' BIRTHDAY PARTIES 101

- Keep the birthday bash as small as possible. Usually between 5 and 10 kids is plenty. I like going by as many children as the birthday child's age. That way, there's no argument.

- Keep it simple. Don't load up on themed napkins, paper plates, cups, or baggies. All that just gets thrown out, and the kids don't care. Save yourself the effort.

- Set a time limit for the party, so that the parents know when to pick up their kids. Nobody wants to be around a bunch of kids crashing on sugar for too long.

- Plan plenty of activities—bored kids are prone to fighting. That doesn't mean you have to rent a jumpy house or hire a pony. The activities can be as simple as a movie and board games.

- Consider cupcakes instead of a more traditional cake. There is nothing more nerve-racking than having all the kids screaming for a piece with a rose. If you get all the cupcakes EXACTLY the same, you'll lessen your chances for meltdowns.

- Skip the goodie bag. I have instituted a "No Presents/No Goodie Bag" policy for birthday parties, and believe it or not, my kids are okay with it. My husband and I buy our kids one really nice gift for their birthday. We tell everybody beforehand that there will be lots of fun but no goodie bags. In lieu of presents, we ask that a donation be made to a children's charity or animal shelter (something the kids can relate to). This is an easy way to get your kids thinking about those less fortunate.

HERE ARE MY REASONS TO SKIP THE PRESENTS

- The parents of the kids invited don't have to rush out in a panic to buy a present, and the parents of the birthday kid don't have to rush out the morning of the party to buy a bunch of crap for the goodie bags.

- You're not stuck with a bunch of ridiculous gifts that you would never buy for your child like the 1,000-piece bead or LEGO kit or, God forbid, a paint set.

- The parents of your guests are not stuck with a bunch of goodie bag crap that they are just going to throw away.

This rule is good for the parents, good for the kids, and good for the earth, since you're not buying useless stuff that just gets thrown out.

FOR THOSE TIMES WHEN YOU JUST HAVE TO GET A GIFT

However, if you just have to buy *something*, here's a list of presents to get the kiddies that are impressive but also good for the planet (and cheap).

- Tickets—to the zoo, a local museum, the movies, a sports event, an ice skating rink

- Bird feeder kit

- Classic paperbacks (used books are fine, as long as they're not too beat up)

- Recycled-paper journal or diary

- Small terra-cotta pots, soil, and seeds make a fun party activity. The kids can take their new plant home and watch it grow (no more goodie bags full of plastic garbage!).

- Grow your own butterfly kit (www.insectlove.com).

GIFT WRAPPING

Keep it as simple as possible. I have one roll of brown craft paper, one package of natural raffia, and one roll of clear tape in my gift-wrapping room. (Technically, my "gift-wrapping room" is my dining room table, but I digress. . . .) I wrap every single gift I send in brown paper with a raffia ribbon. It's elegant and understated, but best of all, these materials are cheap and don't take much room to store. Sometimes I might get crazy and add a sprig of eucalyptus or a small ornament to my wrapping, but that's it.

HERE ARE SOME OTHER UNIQUE GIFT WRAPS THAT YOU MIGHT CONSIDER:

- Comic pages from the Sunday newspaper
- Recycled gift bags from gifts you have received
- Pages from all of those catalogs you get around the holidays
- Recycled aluminum foil
- Old maps
- Reusable shopping bags
- Make two gifts in one:
    * Wrap baby gifts in a baby tub or diaper bag
    * Fill a watering can with gardening supplies
    * Stuff a large mixing bowl or stockpot with utensils
    * Wrap a girlfriend's present in a colorful pashmina or vintage tea towel
- Paper bags
- Old boxes: shoeboxes, cigar boxes, etc.

HALF-ASSED HOSPITALITY— ENTERTAINING FOR BIG PEOPLE

Now that we've covered the most basic necessities for keeping your family fed and cheap ideas to keep your children occupied, let's step out into actual entertaining (with other big people, in nice clothes). I love having people over, but it took me more than a decade to figure out how to do it right. I discovered that no one really cares about all the minute details, they only remember the good time. Remember, these are people you like, people who like you. True hospitality is about making people feel welcome, not intimidating them with your entertaining prowess. Take it down a notch and have a good time.

SIZE MATTERS

You don't have to throw huge bashes. Think about it, do you really need all those people in your house? Consider why you have big parties: Is it because you sincerely have 250 friends that you must see all at the same time, or is it because you want to "host to impress"? If it's the latter, consider smaller gatherings more often. Smaller parties are less work and more enjoyable for the hostess—trust me.

Consider the following fun party ideas for groups of six or fewer:

Poker night ⚹ Throw a length of green felt over the kitchen table. Serve pizza, sodas, and beer.

Magazine club ⚹ Who's got time for a book club? I haven't read a whole book since my daughter was born nine years ago. A magazine article I think I can handle. Invite a few of your girlfriends to read from their favorite rags and share with the group. Make sure there's a nice variety, from *Vanity Fair* to tabloids. Serve a generous cheese and fruit plate with Chardonnay and Pinot Noir.

The backyard barbecue » I particularly love outdoor parties. It keeps people out of the house, and you can just hose down the patio when everyone leaves.

The playdate » If you like any of your kids' friends' parents, invite them over for snacks and conversation. The kids tend to take care of themselves in these situations (mostly), and it's the perfect time to kick back and catch up. Don't fret over the food—I have no problem eating leftover chicken nuggets and cold fries if I can have the kids occupied for a while.

FYI: You'll want to pair these nuggets with a nice Riesling (see page 135).

Oscar party » There's only so much room around the flat screen, so invite just a few of your closest friends. Have everyone dress up and take their photo as they walk in. Serve theater food like pizza, popcorn, nachos, candy, and champagne, of course.

Progressive dinners » These are great. You have appetizers at one house, dinner at another, and dessert at yet another house. There are only so many courses in a meal, so this type of party gets complicated with more than three or four couples. Only involve friends who live close to each other, or you'll spend too much of the night driving around—no fun.

Potluck » These types of dinners can get totally out of control with large groups, but are very manageable with smaller gatherings. You make the main dish and give suggestions to your guests. A simple request of salad, side dish, dessert, or bread will suffice. Trying to get dishes back to people weeks after your dinner is a pain, so I try to shift their food into my dishes early in the evening. That way the table looks cohesive, and I can throw guests' dishes into the dishwasher and return them to their owners before the night is over.

HALF-ASSED INVITATIONS

Forget the written invitations. For God's sake, we are lucky enough to live in a time with Evites. It would be a sin not to take advantage of them. The electronic route is also the "greener" way to send invitations to your friends.

See, you're not *lazy*; you're *eco-friendly*. Be warned, however, that electronic invitations can inadvertently go to people's bulk mail folder. Send your Evites out two weeks before your event. If you haven't received a response from certain guests a week before the party, shoot them an e-mail to make sure they received the invitation.

BTW: Just a personal note from me: If you do intend to send written invitations, please do the world a favor and don't send confetti along for the ride in the envelope. I am still picking tiny bits of foil out of my carpet from a party invitation four years ago.

FORGET THE MATCHY-MATCHY

Contrary to common belief, it is not required to have matching dishes, silverware, glasses, and place mats for every guest. Those perfect tables with all the forks in the right place are just plain intimidating. I prefer a mismatched table; it has more personality. Someone breaks a wineglass almost every time we entertain, so we've ended up with a motley inventory. I feel that as long as everyone *has* a glass, it shouldn't matter if the glasses match. When you think about it, mismatched glasses are easier to tell apart. There's no need to buy those dumb wine charms if everyone has a slightly different setup.

In my own home, I keep a set of white dinner plates and bamboo placemats. I use these items as my tablescape base because they are neutral and go with just about anything. Where I like to mix it up is with the table runners, salad plates, napkins, and centerpieces. These items are relatively cheap, don't take up much storage space, and can totally change the look of your table. Check out flea markets and eBay for unique salad plates, glasses, and silverware. Remember, you're not trying to match here, so consider sets that are not complete and mix them with others.

Consider alternatives for traditional table runners and tablecloths. A cheap canvas paint tarp (found at any paint or hardware store) can serve in place of a more expensive white tablecloth over a buffet table. Burlap is an incredibly inexpensive textile and adds an unexpected layer of texture as a table runner. Newspaper is the classic tablecloth when serving messy foods such as crab legs, clams, or oysters.

MUNCHIES

When your guests arrive, it's nice to hand them a strong drink and a snack, but don't get carried away. Constructing a layered tuna tartar or rolling your own sushi is completely unnecessary. People like comfort food. A nice cheese plate is all you really need to stave off starvation. I usually pick three cheeses, grapes, nuts, olives, salami, and hummus. I serve this with a selection of crackers and pita that I always have on hand.

If you're only serving appetizers and would like to add to the cheese plate, keep it simple or buy premade items from your supermarket deli. You don't have to get too fancy here.

Shrimp cocktail » A nice shrimp cocktail is very easy. Buy frozen, precooked shrimp, cocktail sauce, crackers, and lemon. Serve on a nice platter atop a mound of ice or individually in martini glasses filled with crushed ice.

Prosciutto-wrapped asparagus » This is as easy as steaming the asparagus. (Just don't steam it too much. The spears should remain bright green and shouldn't be too floppy.) Once the asparagus has cooled a bit, wrap each spear with a slice of proscuitto. Proscuitto wrapped around breadsticks is a tasty dish too. Serve with a hard cheese and honey mustard.

Caviar ⚇ Caviar is the gold standard of easy appetizers. You can get decent caviar for less than $20/€15 per jar. Serve with a dollop of sour cream on a sliced baguette. Figure on $1/2$ to 1 oz/15 to 30 g of caviar per guest. Caviar is also a fancy way to dress up a tired-looking deviled egg.

Bacon-wrapped scallops ⚇ This sounds difficult, but the trick is to buy precooked bacon. Wrap each scallop with a piece of precooked bacon. Secure with a toothpick. Rub a little olive oil onto the scallops, and use a sprig of rosemary as a skewer. Broil/grill for about 5 minutes at 400°F/200°C/gas 6. Grind a little pepper over the finished product, and you're done.

Cream cheese and Pickapeppa Sauce ⚇ This is super-easy. Unwrap a package of cream cheese, and place it on a small plate. Pour Pickapeppa over the top. Done. If you can't find Pickapeppa (also called "Jamaican ketchup"), salsa works well, too. Serve with crackers.

Brie, two ways ⚇ For a savory version, spoon a generous amount of sun-dried tomato pesto on top and bake till soft. For a sweet version, pour honey over the top, sprinkle with walnuts, and bake till soft. Serve with sliced Bartlett pears and a nice Port.

M&M's and salted peanuts in a bowl ⚇ Sweet and salty goodness sums it up.

Swedish meatballs ⚇ Find them and the sauce at IKEA. Stab meatballs with fancy toothpicks and place on a fancy plate. If you want to get *really* fancy, serve the meatballs individually in Asian soupspoons.

Rotel dip ⚇ This is a delicacy in the South. It's the perfect comfort food, and no one need know how un-nutritious it is. Melt one package of Velveeta with one can of Rotel tomatoes. Serve with corn chips.

Hot and sour popcorn ⚇ Mix freshly popped popcorn with a dash of salt, cayenne pepper, and a squeeze of fresh lime juice. Shake in the microwave bag and serve.

Chips and varied dips ⚇ You can find dozens of great dips in the deli section of your supermarket: spinach dips, crab dip, salsas, bean dips, and so on. Transfer them from their tacky plastic containers into your nice bowls.

Artichoke-spinach dip ⋈ **Always a hit, and super-easy.**

1 cup/240 ml mayonnaise

1 cup/115 g grated Parmesan cheese

One 14-oz/400-g can artichoke hearts

1 small package frozen chopped spinach

1 cup/115 g shredded cheese, like Monterey Jack

crackers and bread

Preheat the oven to 350°F/180°C/gas 4. Mix together the mayonnaise, Parmesan, artichoke hearts, and spinach. Place in a shallow casserole dish, and cover the top with the shredded cheese. Bake for 15 minutes, or until the top is all bubbly. Serve with crackers and bread.

ASKING FOR HELP

I know this goes against every perfectionist hostess's rule book, but it's really OK to ask your guests to help. I was always the hostess who said, "Oh no, I've got it!" when someone would offer to help. I was also the hostess who never got to see any of my parties. Guests want to help. They feel guilty just sitting around while you're slaving away. Find something for them to do that's easy and won't get them dirty. Setting the table or opening wine bottles is a tiny chore that will take a load off your shoulders.

With that said, if *you* are the guest and your hostess is adamant about you *not* helping, take a cue and hold back your desire to help anyway. There's nothing worse for me as a hostess than to see a guest washing my dirty dishes. Don't get me wrong, I'm appreciative, but by the time the food is eaten, I'm ready to take a break. If I see one of my well-meaning guests slopping away in my kitchen, I'm compelled to go help—even when I don't want to.

PAIRING WINE WITH FOOD

There are a lot of wine snobs out there, and to them I say, "Great. Knock yourself out." Everyone should have a passion. Good for them. I personally don't get it. But I am not here to judge. If you want to have a fancy wine-talking party, do it with gusto. If you just want to have some nice wine with dinner, read on.

My basic rule is that reds go with red meat, and white goes with fish, chicken, and veggies. However, over the years, it's become more difficult to find that perfect pairing as wines and recipes have become more refined. Just remember that regardless of what anybody tells you, there are really no steadfast rules when it comes to wine pairing. The best match is what tastes right to you and your guests.

Nevertheless, if you are afraid you're going to look like a complete idiot at your next soiree, check out the following simple tips for buying and serving wine.

Match the weight of the wine with the weight of the food ✸ **This is pretty straightforward: heavy, spicy dishes should be served with fuller-bodied wines like Cabernet Sauvignon, Chianti, and Merlot, while light dishes such as seafood or stir-fry should be served with lighter wines like Pinot Grigio or Sauvignon Blanc.**

Pairing flavors ✸ **As you begin to pair your wine choices with your menu, think about how the flavors will complement and contrast with one another. A sweeter wine like a Riesling or German Gewürztraminer will make salty dishes even more appealing by contrast, while a crisp, slightly acidic Sauvignon Blanc goes well with spicy foods. A smoky Pinot Noir balances nicely with rich fish dishes like salmon.**

FYI: If you've got some fairly cheap red wine and want to make it taste more expensive, try decanting. This process is as simple as transferring the wine to another container and letting it sit for anywhere from twenty minutes to two hours. The process can add complexity and subtlety. When you decant a bottle of wine, basically two things happen. First, the sediment settles to the bottom and separates from the wine. This is good because the sediment can leave a bitter taste in the wine. Second, the agitation of transferring the wine from one container to another allows oxygen to mix with the wine. This is good because it enables the wine to "breathe." The more oxygen mixes with the wine, the more developed the taste.

A SLAP IN THE FACE TO GENERATIONS OF SOUTHERN LADIES EVERYWHERE

Electronic invitation Web sites usually offer e-mail "thank-you notes" in addition to their selection of invitations. I know what you're thinking: *it doesn't seem right*. It would be in the worst taste imaginable to resort to sending a thank-you note by e-mail. Well, of course it's in bad taste. We all know that. I was raised in the South. I get it: you say please; thank you; yes, ma'am; no, sir; and you better get a handwritten thank-you note (on family crest stationery) out in less than a week, missy.

Obviously, there are situations where a written note of thanks is just plain mandatory, like wedding gift, shower gifts, graduation gifts, gifts from older folks, endowments . . . you get the idea. I'm just saying that there's more than one way to look at this situation. Sometimes you can postpone sending a proper note and then forget about it altogether. It's better to send something subpar than nothing at all. If you find yourself in a jam and you're feeling guilty saying "thanks! :)" via e-mail, consider the eco-friendly excuse: Instead of thinking of yourself as an ungrateful louse as you hit the Send button, imagine yourself instead an eco-friendly trailblazer:

- No chopping down trees

- No contribution to unnecessary bleaches or dyes in our drinking water

- No fossil fuels used in the delivery

- The 21st-century way to show love to your friends *and* the environment

FYI: The "eco-friendly excuse" works well in almost any awkward social situation:

- Forget to wrap the present for your girlfriend's birthday party? You love trees and choose to recycle. *That's* why you brought her gift in a used Happy Meal box.

- The kids look especially dirty on a playdate? You're conserving water.

- Hate to cook? I get out of cooking all summer long by using the "We can't get the kitchen all hot, or we'll waste electricity on the air-conditioning" excuse.

ENTERTAINING MYTHS DEBUNKED

MYTH #1: YOU MUST GO "ALL OUT" ON DECORATIONS.

Let's talk "themes" for a moment. I will admit that for holidays, kids' parties, and dinner parties, I like to prepare with an idea in mind. However, that doesn't mean I'm going to run out to the craft store and buy a bunch of cheesy decorations just for a party. Honestly, most of the decorations purchased at craft stores are as tacky as a tube top. Unless there are very small children attending your event, stay away from the fold-out paper turkeys, small wooden villages, or crepe paper. There's too much work involved in this process, and the results are anticlimactic at best. Simple elegance is what you're going for. Instead of garish decorations, consider subtle elements like the color of your napkins and charger plates, music, and unique centerpieces (see page 143 for a list of easy centerpieces).

MYTH #2: DINNER PARTIES HAVE TO BE "SIT-DOWN" AND FORMAL.

Nonsense. Some of the best parties I've thrown involved a countertop buffet and guests sitting all over the house. People remember the conversation and the good times, not the tablescape.

BUFFET TABLE PREP

- Other than the food, almost everything on the buffet table can be arranged the night before. Save yourself the pressure on party night and prep as early as possible.

- Create the buffet on your countertop, kitchen island, kitchen table, or even your coffee table.

- For more visual interest, use cake stands, stacks of books, or inverted pots to create different levels for the dishes. Place a tablecloth over your "risers," as they will likely be unattractive.

> ⊙ Present the food and serving pieces in an organized manner.
> Start with the plates, napkins, and silverware at the beginning
> of the buffet, followed by the salads, entrées, and bread.

BUFFET THEMES

Taco bar ⋗ Grill some chicken or sauté ground beef or turkey in seasonings. Serve with diced tomatoes, onions, lettuce, shredded cheese, chips, and margaritas. In your half-assed hostess kitchen (see page 104), you should have an array of fancy salsas and tortillas. For décor, grab some terra-cotta pots from the garden and use them as votive holders. Throw a Mexican blanket over your dining table as a tablecloth. You can find thousands of inexpensive Mexican blankets on eBay. I use mine as an extra blanket for my guest room when it's not in use as party décor.

Fourth of July buffet ⋗ You're really only expected to provide hot dogs, hamburgers, and the fixin's here—don't kill yourself. Same goes for décor: a few flags are cute, very patriotic, and *easy*. I keep a few bright, blue metal buckets in my garage. (Blue goes with everything. I got mine at Target, but most home stores sell a variety of colored buckets during the summer months.) For my July 4th party, I use them as ice buckets for beer. They also serve as a centerpiece for my buffet; I fill them with red and white carnations. (Carnations get a bad rap as cheap corsage flowers. They are cheap, but they also smell great and are lovely when bunched together.) Another fun idea for a centerpiece is to fill a bucket with sand. Insert small flags or live sparklers.

Italian buffet ⋗ Keep it simple and serve a pizza or single pasta dish with salad and bread. Most Italian markets sell frozen tiramisu. Pick one up on the way home. (For a homemade touch, whip some fresh cream with confectioners' sugar and vanilla. Dollop on top and add a sprig of mint.) Place a bottle of red and a bottle of white at the end of the buffet table. Because it's hard to pull off a super-elegant look in a half-assed way, I tend to go the way of high camp: a red-checkered tablecloth, an old Chianti bottle/candleholder, and some Dean Martin or Connie Francis playing in the background.

The Low Country boil » A Southern classic. This yummy one-pot dish is a combination of sausage, crab legs, shrimp, corn on the cob, and potatoes. The beauty of the recipe is you can play around with it. Leave out the things you don't like, and double up on the things you do like. Cover your buffet table in old newspaper, and let your guests help themselves right out of the pot. Serve with cocktail sauce, lemons, crackers, LOTS of napkins, and ice-cold beer.

4 lb/1.8 kg new potatoes (the very small ones)
5 qt/4.7 L water
1 bag crab boil seasoning
Old Bay seasoning
2 lb/910 g kielbasa or hot links
6 ears corn, broken in half
4 lb/1.8 kg large fresh shrimp/prawns (Most people leave the shell
    on, but it's WAY messier. Buy them shelled if you can.)
3 lb/1.4 kg whole crab, broken into small pieces

To prepare, add the potatoes to a really big pot, then add the water and the seasonings. Cover the pot and heat to a rolling boil; cook for 5 minutes. Add the kielbasa and corn, and return to a boil. Cook for 10 minutes or until potatoes are tender. Next, add the shrimp and crab to the pot; cook for 3 to 4 minutes or until the shrimp turn pink. Drain.

The dessert buffet ✳ This is the perfect occasion to go potluck (more on that to follow). Everyone has a dessert recipe. Have your guests bring their favorite, and serve with coffee, tea, and dessert liquors. Here are two easy dessert recipes that KILL every time.

EASY APPLE TART WITH JACK DANIELS ICE CREAM

FOR THE ICE CREAM
1 container vanilla ice cream
1 bottle Jack Daniels

FOR THE TART
frozen puff pastry
fresh apples
sugar
cinnamon

To prepare the ice cream, soften the vanilla ice cream and mix with the whiskey in a large bowl. The amount of whiskey is entirely up to you, but I add about 1 cup/240 ml. Let it set overnight before serving with the tart.

To prepare the tart, unwrap the puff pastry and place on a greased cookie sheet/baking tray. Pinch the edges so that it forms a ridge around all four sides. Peel and slice the apples, and place on top of the pastry. Sprinkle with sugar and cinnamon. Bake in the oven at 350°F/180°C/gas 4 until the pastry browns and the apples are bubbly.

MOTHER FEAR'S NEVER-FAIL COOKIES

one 12-oz/340-g package chocolate chips
one 8-oz/225-g package chopped walnuts or pecans
one 19-oz/540-g package chocolate chunk cookie dough (the roll is fine,
    but I prefer the dough that is precut into cookie-size squares)

To prepare, pull out a plastic cutting board and sprinkle a healthy portion of chocolate chips and nuts on top. Roll each serving of cookie dough in the mixture until completely coated. Bake the cookies according to the instructions on the package. These "doctored up" cookies taste exactly like homemade. People go CRAZY over them, and no one needs to know how easy they were to make.

MYTH #3: YOU HAVE TO COOK EVERYTHING.

Potluck dinners are great. Like I said before, your guests want to do something to help. If your inner Joan Crawford can't stand the thought of an unknown menu and mismatched casserole dishes all over the kitchen, ask for specifics that won't interfere with your master plan. People are happy to bring salad, dessert, bread, or alcohol.

The potluck piece-together » Instead of having your guests bring a casserole or complicated dessert, have them bring the *ingredients* for a dish that you can prepare once everyone has arrived. This works best with easy-to-assemble dishes like burritos, tacos, burgers, and pizza. The trick is to invite people you can trust. A taco dinner isn't the same without the tortillas your sister promised to bring, but didn't.

MYTH #4: CENTERPIECES HAVE TO BE FANCY.

Have you ever been to a dinner party where the centerpiece was so tall and extravagant that you couldn't see the person across from you? You'd have to lean around it to have a conversation? Keep it simple.

HERE ARE SOME CLEVER IDEAS FOR IMPROMPTU CENTERPIECES:

⊙ Buy a tray of wheatgrass at your local health food store (around $20/€15). Cut into wide strips and use the grass as a natural, simple table runner. Place votive candles and flowers in the grass for added pizzazz.

⊙ A row of votive candles is an inexpensive centerpiece and complements everyone's complexion. I like to place my candles in antique sugar molds I've collected over the years. You can find molds at Napastyle.com or on eBay. These vintage molds have an elegant rustic appearance and add charm to any table. An alternative is to place the candles in small brown paper bags. Just make sure that the bags are large enough that the flames don't touch the paper. You want people talking about your party for years to come, but not because you burned the house down.

⊙ Float candles and flowers from the garden in a shallow bowl.

⊙ I keep a dozen or so small potted succulents in my garden. I "plant" them in a row down my dining table for an instant centerpiece. Succulents are inexpensive, beautiful, come in a variety of colors and shapes, and are almost impossible to kill.

⊙ Fruits and vegetables aren't just on the menu; they make great centerpieces. Artichokes, pears, green apples—arranged on a long serving tray, these edibles make a simple, architectural statement. Fill small clear vases with water and whole lemons. Place fresh daisies into the lemon-filled vases. This look SCREAMS springtime.

⊙ A long piece of driftwood makes a beautiful centerpiece for your table.

⊙ Use unexpected kitchen items as tablescape décor. Consider using tin vegetable cans as vases for small bunches of flowers. A fancy colander makes a whimsical statement as a container for a floral centerpiece. Just make sure the flowers are already in a vase before they're placed in the colander. Nobody wants the centerpiece leaking all over the table.

- **Turn all those cheap, clear glass vases under your sink into hurricane lamps for all seasons. I place long taper candles in the vases, then secure the candles by filling the vase halfway with various materials. Let your imagination be your guide to finding the right "fillers" for your lamps. Here are some of the materials I've used for various occasions:**

  * Girls' night in—Good & Plenty candies (they look like the pills from *Valley of the Dolls*)
  * Valentine's Day—candy hearts and bright red candles
  * Summer—sand and small shells
  * Halloween—candy corn
  * Autumn—acorns, unpopped popcorn in various colors
  * Christmas—small tree ornaments
  * New Year's—ibuprofen

MYTH #5: YOU MUST HAVE A FULLY STOCKED BAR.

Spending the night bartending is not a great way to enjoy a party, unless, of course, you have a tip jar. A few bottles of red, a few bottles of white, and a "signature drink" is all I ever do anymore. You can buy large jars with "taps" at the bottom at most home stores. Fill the jar with premade mojitos, sangria, lemon drops, whatever you like. Guests can serve themselves, saving you a lot of work. These awesomely easy cocktails will both amaze and intoxicate.

. . . .

JAMAL'S APRICOT MINT JULEP

pinch of fresh mint
dash of simple syrup
dash of apricot liqueur
2 oz/55 ml Maker's Mark
club soda

To prepare, muddle the mint, simple syrup, and apricot liqueur in a rocks glass. Top with ice, and add the Maker's Mark. Add a splash of club soda to finish.

SWEETIE'S LIKELY 2.0

2 oz/55 ml spiced rum
2 oz/60 ml coconut rum
20 oz/600 ml pineapple juice
splash of orange juice

To prepare, pour all of the ingredients (in order) into a rocks or Collins glass. (I have collection of vintage tiki glasses I use.) This is the easiest drink ever and great on a hot summer day.

ROSEMARY LEMON DROP

2 oz/55 ml lemon vodka
1 oz/30 ml limoncello
$1/2$ oz/15 ml triple sec
splash of rosemary simple syrup (marinate fresh rosemary sprigs
    in the syrup overnight)
superfine/castor sugar for rimming the martini glasses
sprig of rosemary or lemon twist for garnish

To prepare, mix all the ingredients except the superfine sugar and rosemary sprig with ice in a shaker glass. Shake and strain into a martini glass rimmed in sugar. Add the small rosemary sprig as a garnish.

MAMACITA'S MEXICAN MARTINI

It is very important to use the finest ingredients in this drink. If the booze is cheap and the juice is from a can, the drink will be terrible.

2 oz/55 ml tequila (don't cheap out here; I suggest Patrón or better)
1 oz/30 ml Cointreau orange liqueur or Grand Marnier
1 oz/30 ml freshly squeezed lime juice
1 oz/30 ml simple syrup
splash of freshly squeezed orange juice
salt for rimming the martini glass
lime twist for garnish

To prepare, pour all of the ingredients except the salt and lime twist into a large cocktail shaker filled with ice. Shake and strain into a salt-rimmed martini glass. Garnish with the lime twist.

SOUTHERN SIPPIN' PUNCH

one 750 ml bottle Southern Comfort
1 can frozen lemonade, thawed
12 oz/360 ml freshly squeezed orange juice
juice from 6 lemons
2 L lemon-lime soda or ginger ale
lemon and orange slices for garnish

To prepare, chill the whiskey, lemonade, orange juice, and lemon juice, then mix them together in a punch bowl. When ready to serve, add the soda and garnish with the citrus slices.

NOT HOMEMADE AT ALL

My favorite thing to make for dinner is reservations.

— UNKNOWN

One of the best parties I ever attended was a Kentucky Derby party thrown by a friend of a friend. It was a catered affair. Female guests were asked to wear their fanciest hats, while gentlemen wore seersucker and suspenders. Waiters and bartenders dressed in crisp white aprons served authentic Southern mint juleps in real silver cups while an amateur bookie took bets in the front parlor. But here's what made the party so memorable: the food was all from Kentucky Fried Chicken. It was pure wit to have passed hors d'oeuvres from a fast-food restaurant. It just goes to show that you don't have to slave over a stove all day to throw a party people will talk about for years.

Takeout is the perfect solution for the half-assed hostess's dinner party. Unlike Sandra Lee and her "Semi-Homemade," consider not homemade at all. My trick is to simply dump takeout into my fabulously eclectic collection of bowls and platters. Don't even be apologetic about it. Hell, leave the containers out. If I feel like I've got to do something, I will garnish my plates with edible flowers and herbs, so that the presentation doesn't look too half-assed.

 Costco buffet ✧ I'm not kidding you—Costco has good stuff. It's the containers that look cheesy and cheap. Transfer it all over to your own fancy plates, platters, and bowls. Check out the premade food aisle. Vegetable trays, salads, and full-on dinners are all there—ready to go and cheap.

Chinese/Vietnamese/Thai food ❧ Soups, sate skewers, rice dishes, and noodle dishes are easy to keep warm until company arrives. Choose uncooked rice-paper spring rolls instead of fried egg rolls; fried foods get soggy too quickly. Transfer the takeout onto your nice plates and bowls, and serve with Chinese soup-spoons and chopsticks. Place spring rolls on a bed of cilantro atop a nice platter for that "I made this from scratch" look. Sake is cheap and a fun alternative to the more traditional red and white wines.

Pizza ❧ This is the easiest—just order delivery. Stock the bar with mid-ranged Chiantis and Pinot Grigio. Invest in a red-checked tablecloth. Rent *The Godfather*. Play Dean Martin, Frank Sinatra, Perry Como, and Connie Francis.

Mexican food ❧ Always have a gourmet salsa in the house. Serve with chips, chipotle hummus, and avocado slices as an appetizer. Takeout tamales, beans, and rice are easy to keep warm until guests arrive. Most Mexican restaurants also carry some sort of fish ceviche. You want to make sure and buy ceviche the day of the party—no earlier. Keep the container in the fridge until guests arrive. Place portions in martini or margarita glasses and garnish with a slice of avocado. For a kitschy twist on a Cinco de Mayo party, just run to a local taqueria. Grab some tacos and burritos. As long as the margaritas are good and strong, no one will care that it's takeout. Forget the authentic Mexican décor; brightly colored salad plates, colorful napkins, woven napkin rings, and a succulent centerpiece will get the message across. After the party, plant the succulents outdoors in partial sun.

Indian food ⊳ Curries, rice dishes, naan, and samosas are easy to keep warm till the guests arrive. To save money, keep dried jasmine and saffron rice in your pantry and make your own. Consider broiling a flank steak or lamb cubes and briefly simmering in a pint of red curry sauce from the restaurant. An order of dal (a soupy lentil dish), served over rice, is a yummy side dish. Setting the mood for this evening is key: low lighting, lots of candles, and the right music (see my suggestions on page 150).

 Japanese ⊳ Sushi rolls keep better than regular sushi. That doesn't mean that they can stay refrigerated forever, so pick up the sushi right before the guests arrive. After about an hour in the fridge, the fish will develop a "skin" and the rice will get hard. Miso soup is the perfect appetizer. Most sushi bars will sell it by the quart. See my quick and easy Chicken Teriyaki recipe on page 114. Serve with chopsticks, hot tea, and sake.

HEY, MR. DJ, PLAY A SONG FOR ME

In my opinion, music can make or break the mood of any gathering. If your menu steers you toward a theme, consider music that complements the food. I always use music as the major player in my party decorating scheme.

Lucky for me, I have a good friend who is an awesome DJ. Lucky for you, I plan to share his wealth of information regarding CDs for theme entertaining. (I'm sure you can get most of this on iTunes as well.)

SOUTH OF THE BORDER
Trio Los Panchos, *De Colección 20*; Juan Garcia Esquivel, *Cabaret Mañana* and *Space-Age Bachelor Pad Music*; Héctor Lavoe, *El Cantante: The Originals*; various artists, *Putumayo Presents: Latin Lounge*

INDIAN AND MIDDLE EASTERN
Kama Sutra soundtrack; Ravi Shankar and Philip Glass, *Passages*; Ravi Shankar, *Live at Monterey*; J Boogie, *J Boogie's Dubtronic Science*; ARABesque, *The Compilation* (Gut Records)

JAPANESE
Kohachiro Miyata, *Shakuhachi: The Japanese Flute*; Ryuichi Sakamoto, *Beauty*

CUBAN
Francisco Cespedes and Gonzalo Rubalcaba, *Con el Permiso de Bola*; Ry Cooder and Buena Vista Social Club, *Buena Vista Social Club*

BRAZILIAN
Milton Nascimento Jobim Trio, *Novas Bossas*; Seu Jorge, *The Life Aquatic Studio Sessions*

IRISH
The Chieftans, *The Celtic Harp*

AFRICAN
Ali Farka Toure with Ry Cooder, *Talking Timbuktu*; Youssou N'Dour, *The Guide (Wommat)*

ITALIAN
The Big Night soundtrack; Connie Francis, *Connie Francis Sings Italian Favorites*

FRENCH
Various artists, *Putamayo Presents: French Café*

CHINESE
Various artists, *Chinoiserie*

Newspaper ≫ A great makeshift tablecloth for casual dinners and cookouts.

Tea towels ≫ I like to place a nice tea towel over each dining chair. They are easier to clean and less austere than cloth napkins, and they are more charming than a paper towel.

Hair dryer ≫ You buy roses for your party and they won't open. What's a panicked hostess to do? Fill the vase with warm water. If that doesn't work, blow-dry the buds on the low setting.

A large wooden butcher block ≫ I only use plastic cutting boards for actual cutting. They are easier to clean and don't harbor bacteria like wood can. That said, butcher blocks make lovely serving platters for cheese plates, fruit, breads, and crackers.

Salt ≫

- Extinguishes grease fires. Never throw water on a grease fire.

- Cleans silver in minutes. Line a glass casserole dish with aluminum foil. Fill with warm water, baking soda/bicarbonate of soda, and salt. Place your tarnished silver in the water. Minutes later, you have perfectly clean silver without the rubbing and buffing.

- Keeps cheese fresher longer. Wrapping cheese in cheesecloth dampened with salt water will prevent the cheese from getting moldy.

- Keeps food from discoloring. Apple and potato slices won't turn brown if you cover them in salt water.

- Use for easy disposal of bacon grease. Grease can clog your kitchen drain. Instead, pour warm bacon grease into a cup lined with aluminum foil. Once the grease has solidified, pull out the foil, wrap, and throw away.

- Removes grunge from your grill. Wad up some aluminum foil and rub it across your grill grate. It will remove all the old, burned food.

- Makes a great makeshift funnel. Just form into the shape of a funnel. It works really well.

Grocery store delivery ✻ Most chain grocery stores offer a free delivery service. If you can get your act together to come up with a list, delivery will save you hours a week.

Multidisc CD players and iPods ✻ There's nothing worse than looking up from your party and noticing there's been no music for God knows how long. You're too busy to play DJ. Line up your CDs before the party, and load them up in a multidisc player. If you have an iPod, make sure it's ready to go before the guests arrive.

Bagged salad greens ✻ It's all chopped, washed, and ready to go.

Precut vegetables ✻ Same as above—a total time-saver. The precut onions are the best—no tears.

Floating candles ✻ Bathrooms in older homes can be less than inviting. Old grout, worn enamel, and overall grunginess can be embarrassing when entertaining. Fill your tub and place loads of floating candles inside. The glow from the candles will be enough for folks to take care of business, but the room will be dark enough to disguise flaws. Candles add ambience and make *any* room look better.

Fancy toothpicks ✻ Just about everything looks gourmet on a long, fancy toothpick: cherry tomatoes, meatballs (IKEA sells the best frozen meatballs), shrimp, dates, figs, even chicken nuggets for a kids' dinner.

Vodka in the freezer ⊱ Instant martinis, neither shaken nor stirred.

Frozen puff pastry ⊱ Cheap and keeps forever in the freezer. Use it as the "wrapping" for savory appetizers and desserts.

Easy Mac instant macaroni and cheese ⊱ Seriously, a hot meal in SIX MINUTES?!?! Let's face it: There were our lives *before* Easy Mac, and our lives *after* this time-saving, delicious kids' staple.

REALITY CHECK ON HOSTESS GIFTS

S ince when did it become necessary to bring more than a bottle of wine to a party? All the style mavens these days say that if you truly want to impress your hostess, you should bring picture frames or guest books or candlesticks or wooden wine boxes with fancy openers and bottle stoppers. I don't know about you, but having to go out and *shop* in exchange for a free meal doesn't seem right. The other thing to consider is that maybe the hostess doesn't want all that crap. A bottle of wine is fine. A bottle of liquor is quicker.

THE HALF-ASSED (HOUSEGUEST) HOSTESS

Twelve years ago, my husband and I moved to Northern California. We feel extremely fortunate to raise our kids in one of the most beautiful areas of our country. Because of our proximity to so much fabulousness, we get a pretty regular stream of guests from back home. When you love having friends and family around, it's more important to show your hospitality than to kill yourself trying to impress.

As a rule, I always throw one nice dinner party or barbecue while my guests are in town. It's a wonderful time to catch up and introduce your old friends to your new friends. After that, I need my guests to be fairly independent. Between the two kids and the two jobs, I never have the time I would like to spend with them. Thus, the following half-assed houseguest guidelines.

THE INVITATION

Be clear with your invitation. Invite guests for a certain amount of time, and make sure you are all clear on the departure day. You'll save yourself the drama by diplomatically letting your company know ahead of time when the party's over. Once the invitation is extended, it's nice to send your guests an e-mail with information they will need for packing. Let them know what the weather will be like and if they need to bring any special clothes for events you have planned. If you can pick them up from the airport, great. If you *cannot* pick them up from the airport, be sure to let them know ahead of time.

CREATE THE SPACE

If you have a fully appointed guest room in your home, good for you! You are more than halfway there. Skip over to the end of this section, and take a load off.

For the rest of us who don't have a designated room for visitors, it can be a real challenge to ensure comfort and privacy for both you and your guests. If you only have one bathroom, the challenge can seem insurmountable.

DOUBLE-DUTY ROOMS

Rooms that serve more than one purpose are the only answer for the square-foot-challenged half-assed houseguest hostess, but I have a few rules and suggestions:

If you can, avoid using the public areas of your house for guests. It just doesn't work. As much as you might think that the sleeper sofa in the family room is perfect for guests, it burdens everyone involved. The guest has no privacy and no control over his or her bedtime. You might have someone in the full throes of jet lag, with no other choice than to sit on the "bed" while two screaming children watch "just one more" *SpongeBob*. You, on the other hand, will have to avoid that centrally located room altogether for fear that you might accidentally see your brother-in-law naked and never be able to speak to him again.

Most people do the old home office/guest room scenario. This can work well, because most rooms, no matter how small, will accommodate a small desk and a futon. However, this setup will be a disaster if you actually need to *use* your office during your guest's stay. Your company will feel uncomfortable having you traipsing in and out all day, and you don't want to feel weird about working. If you have a portable computer, the answer may be to set up a small makeshift office somewhere else in the house. Take the bare necessities and set up in your bedroom, kitchen, or dining room.

Then there are the kids' rooms. This can be tricky, as you don't want your kids to feel ripped off every time a guest arrives. My kids are still young enough to accept a small bribe in exchange for the use of their rooms. We have "camping nights" when we have company. The kids move out of their rooms the day before the guests arrive, so I can wash the sheets and tidy up a bit. We put the kids in the family room in sleeping bags, have fun snacks, and let them watch TV a little later than usual. Works every time.

As for the bathroom . . . If you have two, great. Let your guests know which one they'll be using right off the bat. If you only have one, be clear about your morning schedule, so there is no confusion and frustration.

Once you've picked the perfect spot for your visitors, you'll need to clean. Check out my speed-cleaning checklist on page 41.

SHOW THEM THE ROPES (BUT DON'T GET CRAZY)

All the magazines say you should find out what kind of foods your guests like, if they have any food allergies or dietary restrictions, and so on. I pretty much disagree with all of that. I find that when I ask people what they need, they always say, "Oh, nothing. I'll be fine." But when they get here, they're like, "So where do you keep your hazelnut nondairy creamer?" I choose instead to escort my visitors to the nearest grocery store once they've had a chance to settle in. That way they can get whatever extras they need themselves. They don't have to feel like they've inconvenienced me, and I don't have to worry about what to buy.

They also say that you should provide your guests with all the information and brochures they might need concerning local attractions, sporting events, museums, and the like. I say that's what the Internet is for. Give your guests some general information, and let them know that they are free to use your computer at any time.

Give a quick informational tour of the house and any "house rules" (like the cat does not get to go outside, and Junior does not get two desserts on Tuesdays). Make sure your guests know they can eat or drink anything they want. Show them where you keep the extra towels and toilet paper.

Most adult guests do not need to be coddled. Give them a key to your house so that they can come and go as they please. If you use a security system, make sure they know the codes.

AMENITIES

Make sure that your guests feel welcome and comfortable in their new digs. A few thoughtful touches will make even the most unconventional setup more inviting. The sheets should be clean and the bed made (even if the bed is a sofa). I have a large basket with handles that I keep in my closet. It contains two fluffy white towels, two washcloths, a terry cloth robe, a hair dryer, two bottles of water, Q-tips, and a selection of high-end soaps and lotions. The basket has a very spa-like appeal and is easy to manage. I just plop the basket on my guests' bed and know that they're taken care of for the duration of their stay.

EPILOGUE

My Last Rant,
and Then You Can Be On Your Way

Okay, so you're on your deathbed (we're switching gears here, hang on). What are your regrets? That your parties weren't the toniest? That your home was never clean enough? Are you lying there just *kicking yourself* for not hemming those café curtains on your way out the door to the hospital? One can only hope not.

Take a look at your life—do you like what you see? Live every day like it's the last one. Find a passion, not an OCD. No drama allowed. Don't worry about all the toys; just hold your kids and smooch them on their perfect little heads. Embrace the chaos. Quit trying to keep up with the Joneses and tell those jealous bitches to suck it. Give yourself some credit. Do less and enjoy more. Wave your hands in the air like you just don't care. Put down the glue gun and step away, ma'am.

Listen, if I'm able to convince just one other mom out there to take herself a little less seriously a little more often, then I've succeeded at what I set out to do.